Anatomy
of a Gangster

Also by Gary Levine:

*The Car Solution: The Steam Engine
Comes of Age*

Anatomy of a Gangster

Jack "Legs" Diamond

Gary Levine

SOUTH BRUNSWICK AND NEW YORK: A. S. BARNES AND COMPANY
LONDON: THOMAS YOSELOFF LTD

A. S. Barnes and Co., Inc.
Cranbury, New Jersey 08512

Thomas Yoseloff Ltd
Magdalen House
136–148 Tooley Street
London SE1 2TT, England

Library of Congress Cataloging in Publication Data

Levine, Gary
    Anatomy of a gangster.

    Includes index.
    1. Diamond, John, 1895 or 6–1931.   2. Crime and criminals
—United States—Biography.   I. Title.
HV6248.D48L48 1979   364.1′092′4 [B]   78–55448
ISBN 0–498–02246–3

PRINTED IN THE UNITED STATES OF AMERICA

I dedicate this book to my aunt Dorothy Schoicket

"Dotty," as she was affectionately known, was a remarkable person with much inner drive. She was an able business woman, a devoted wife and mother who raised two sons, a strong influence in her family of three sisters and one brother. She was the one the family came to on joyous holidays and in time of trouble. We miss her very much.

Contents

Acknowledgments

There have been many people who have contributed much to this book. My indebtedness to those who were close to Legs Diamond, or who knew much about his activities, is great. I also owe much to those individuals who furnished me with rare photographs of the gangster's activities. I extend special thanks to Dewey Lawrence, Francis Hillfrank, Howard Rice, Marvin Parks, Harry Fritz, Lyle Simpson, Lloyd Tice, George Klein, Phillip Thomas, Jimmy Wynne, Frank Murphy, Joseph Schrowang, Al Gruber, Harry Morrison, Lillian Cornelius, Harry Coale, Duane Murphy, Arthur DuMond and Kurt Wachenheim. I am also grateful to the New York State Police and to the staffs of the New York Public Library Annex, Free Library of Philadelphia, and the New York State Library at Albany.

Introduction

Anatomy of a Gangster, would never have been written without the cooperation of many. State troopers who knew Diamond opened their own collections and gave many interviews. Diamond's friends spoke openly of their association with him and his comrades. And so many people from different backgrounds who knew the gangster well shared information with me. I thank them for their assistance.

There were several instances where a few individuals wanted their names kept secret. And there were individuals who refused to talk, because they did not want to bring back the past or because they did not want their names associated with former crimes.

On one occasion I was driven deep into the Catskill mountains on a winding dirt road that came to a dead end. High atop a mountain, in an isolated cabin, I spoke to a man who had taken care of Diamond's Acra estate and who recalled many aspects of the gangster's life that no one had ever known. I even participated in a search for one of his buried victims and examined an old Lincoln sedan, reputedly owned by him. One time I inspected the site of a brewery, an important source for Diamond's beer, that had been raided by prohibition agents. Another time I was introduced to a close aide of Diamond, who acted as a bodyguard and chauffeur for his wife in 1929, and he was able to recall many details about Diamond's activities that were never known. He had been present once when there was an intrusion by enemy gangsters on the Acra estate.

Several interviews with a part-time chauffeur who worked for Diamond, during the December 1931 kidnapping trial, proved especially important. According to his statements, Diamond had gotten to at least one juror and this influenced the verdict.

The New York City, Albany, and Philadelphia newspapers proved especially important for their contemporary attitudes and opinions about him, and for their frequent write-ups on his activities. Also, such magazines as *The Literary Digest*, *The Saturday Evening Post*, and *Colliers* proved invaluable for their discussion of the gangster problem in America.

While preparing the manuscript, I gathered a large number of photographs of Diamond, his associates, state police activities, road houses, and stills. I also collected many cartoons published in magazines and newpapers that depicted his crimes. Probably no other gangster was photographed so much, and it is through these pictures that one can get an intimate look into a gangster's life.

The slight figure of Jack "Legs" Diamond had a powerful impact on prohibition era crime, especially on bootlegging, drug peddling, and gang warfare. His life time included the period of violent city gangs such as the Whyos and the Five-Pointers, to the gangsters of the twenties and thirties. Throughout he was always in the public eye. The public loved gangsters for many reasons, but primarily because they were self-reliant, diligent, successful, and romantic individualists who were always persecuted by the establishment. But gangsters were really opposed to individualism and would never tolerate independent thought or criticism. If anything they were fascists who had to have their way, something the public did not want to see or could not understand. In fact little was known about the criminal during this period and their anti-social behavior was viewed in terms of bad influences and attitudes. In reality, though, many prominent gangsters had definable personalities, being true psychopaths.

If anything captured the public's imagination it was gangster exploits that were as exciting as those of any figure from the world of fiction and, in many cases, as unbelievable. Legs Diamond lived a more exciting life than any gangster of that period. One afternoon, in the fall of 1930, he took five bullets, two of which went through his chest and two through his left side, yet survived to be shot down on two other occasions. Diamond would eventually be shot down five times, the fifth time being fatal. Throughout all the shootings, the press called him a "clay pigeon" and the public believed he could not be killed.

Diamond also became, for a brief period, heir to the powerful Arnold Rothstein organization. To maintain control over this vast empire, he had to engage in continual warfare with other gangsters and this resulted in many deaths. "Do you know what Legs Diamond was trying to do?" an associate of his asked during an interview. "Well, he was trying to control all of the illicit activities in the East. He was trying to be as big as Capone." For this he was challenged and harrassed by the federal prosecutor of New York City, the Attorney General of the State of New York, Governor Franklin Roosevelt, several European governments including the Prussian state government, which he sued, and other upholders of the law. Even at his home in Acra, he was molested. For a brief period, Greene County was taken over by state troopers, his Acra home was raided several times, and the area was the scene of a massive search for one of his victims.

He was flashy, cocky, sometimes loud, and always deadly. The newspapers painted him as a killer and kingpin in crime. The public saw him as a champion against the dries. But both knew little about his drug operations and what they were doing to America.

The real truth about Legs Diamond lies between the pages of this book.

Anatomy
of a Gangster

I

A Hero is Born

The breeding ground of the prohibition era gangster was the big-city ghetto, where the unassimilated immigrants of Europe and Asia lived. Typical of such places was the Five Points district of New York City, where forty thousand vagrant and destitute children eked out an existence. Reportedly they were too ragged, dirty, and diseased to even be admitted to the public schools. Their homes were "in the dens and stews of the city where thieves, vagabonds, murderers, and gamblers lived."

By the 1890s many of the great Eastern cities were bulging from the almost daily arrivals of the immigrants who swelled the ghettos with their growing numbers. Philadelphia's Kensington and Port Richmond sections, where the Irish-American gangsters Jack and Eddie Diamond grew to manhood, were already overpopulated by 1870. With their wooden clapboard houses, dingy ginmills, back alleys, and cobblestone streets they became home for thousands of Poles, Irish, Lithuanians, and Jews who toiled at menial jobs in the city's industries.

It was the Irish, though, who had the most impact on the city's later development. Their struggle for recognition was difficult and bloody. Philadelphia, as far as they were concerned, was a city of "brotherly love" in name only. Riots against Negroes, anti-abolitionists, and the Irish occurred often in the period before the Civil War, and most of the time the Irish got the worst of it. It was in Philadelphia that the Native American party, the Know-Nothings, and other anti-Catholic and anti-Irish groups held power and dictated policy.

The Irish, "the largest foreign born group for fifty years," had a tremendous impact on the political and business life of the city. Their prosperity can be traced back to the Civil War, where many profited from Philadelphia's position as an important industrial port city and the largest staging area for troops and supplies in the North. As the Irish middle class grew so did the crime and slum problems that stigmatized the group. A large number of street gangs and organizations roamed the streets, the most notable being the Fenians and Schuykill Rangers and they perpetuated the stereotype of the "Irish as alien, sinister, erratic, and incorrigible malefactors." In a short period of time they had alienated themselves from the broader community and had endangered their relationship with their own kind.

Life, in the Port Richmond section, was hard for those newcomers who had not tasted the prosperity around them. The rural Irish, so culturally different, found themselves in an urban environment where they had many obstacles to overcome. Surrounded by long-standing institutions, firmly entrenched businesses, and influential upper-class Protestant families, the Irish moved cautiously toward assimilation. By 1875 they were numerous and influential enough to prompt the mayor to sit in the reviewing stand during the St. Patrick's Day parade.

If the Irish were successful at anything it was in fostering the growth of Catholicism and politics. Churches sprang up everywhere and an aggressive Catholicism daringly competed with a stiff-necked Protestantism. For the majority of Protestants, though, the Irish Catholics were guilty of plotting against American institutions and were "inherently disloyal."

In city politics they pushed ahead, giving birth to the big-city machine. They built up, through the gin mill and fire company, a strong grass roots political organization that by 1895 had a considerable impact on the Democratic Party, but did not dominate either the Democrats or the Republicans in the late nineteenth century.

All was not well, despite the fact that by the end of the century newly built three-family houses signaled the success of the Irish middle class. Unemployment, crime, and poverty were still very much in evidence and the weak quickly perished. Such conditions were burned deeply into Jack and Eddie Diamond, whose parents were very poor. Sara, Jack's mother, was a gentle woman with an aura of beauty and breeding not usually seen in someone of such humble background. She was five feet five inches tall, very slim and had flaming red hair. The few who remembered her remarked how bright she was and how she made all the decisions for the family. "She was a God-fearing woman who never feared hard work," said one neighbor. She had met her husband at a dance in Kilrush, Ireland, and they were married two years later. The crushing poverty of Ireland, the limited chance for a future there, and the threat of food shortages made her realize that America was their only chance. In the fall of 1891, after many months of preparation, they arrived in Philadelphia and were received by her husband John's relatives.

It did not take Sara long to see all the opportunities in her newly adopted country. She was especially impressed by the free public schools and the great industries that abounded everywhere. Although trapped by her lack of schooling, she insisted that Jack and Eddie find something to do with their lives that would be better than working in the sweat shops or at the docks. She admonished, pleaded, and threatened Jack to work hard day and night, to become a success. She constantly cited to him examples of success that she was told of, in her new land, such as James Gordon Bennett, the newspaper magnate, Peter Cooper, the businessman, and Chaunncy Jerome, the clockmaker.

Legs never seemed impressed with success stories and certainly did not let school influence him. The truant officer was often at the Diamond's door and Sara, suffering from excruciating arthritic pain, could not run after her beloved Jack. Only after Board of Education threats to commit Jack to a special school did his attendance become regular.

Beautiful little Sara's health failed, she was stooped over and could no longer hold silverware or pots in her hands, and had many sleepless nights. The common remedies for arthritis then were morphine and heroin, which were readily available, and Sara took them in large doses. Her husband, unable to bear the sight of his wife in such a deplorable condition, was usually away at some ginmill, dead drunk.

John Diamond was never a perfect husband. He was born in Ireland of humble parents and, like his wife, had a poverty-stricken childhood. A short thin man, who frequently coughed from an unknown lung condition, he was never able to elevate himself from the menial jobs that he supported his family with. Within a few weeks of his arrival in Philadelphia, he took a position as a cook in an Irish inn and after a dispute with the owner went from one job to another. Eventually he became a boiler-maker, a helper in a carriage-maker's shop, and finally a packer in a coffee-roasting plant. After spending most of his evenings at one or more of the popular taverns, extolling the virtues of good beer and the Democratic party, he had little time for his two sons.

His greatest achievement was to become a committeeman of the 25th district, in the 31st ward, where he spent much time buying drinks and influencing voters. He would always remember the role he played in the presidential campaign of 1896 that pitted the Republican, William McKinley, against the Democrat, William Jennings Bryan. As a loyal Democrat he pledged himself to work for Bryan, although he was unclear of the issues, especially that of free silver. Going from door to door he pleaded with his Irish kinsmen to vote for Bryan and to read *Coin's Financial School*, a bit of Democratic propaganda. His efforts bore little fruit, for only a few wards went Democratic, with McKinley winning the city and the election.

The Diamond family eventually settled at 2350 East Albert Street, where Jack was born in 1897. He was delivered by a midwife, as was the custom among the poor Irish, and the birth was not recorded in the city records. In fact, it has been estimated that thirty percent of births were not recorded at that time because of omissions by midwives and doctors, who made deliveries in private homes.

As a young boy, Jack was usually in some kind of trouble. He often frequented a discarded marine boiler on a vacant lot that was the home of a group of toughs, known as the Boiler Gang. Pilfering wagons and small warehouses they were constantly harrassed by the police, who already recognized Jack as a notorious tough. As he grew into manhood it became clear that he disliked heavy manual labor. He lasted only a short time on the lesser jobs at the spinning mills, steel mills, and ship yards. His slight build may have contributed to this, as he was only five feet nine inches tall and weighed only 145 pounds. His soft white hands, well-groomed hair, manicured nails, and contralto voice clearly set him apart from the typical burly laborer. But it was the chip on his shoulder and his contempt for authority that made him a hardbitten thug. He could not get along well with bosses and was known to always have a knife or club nearby. He earned his nickname, "Legs," from his nimble and incomparable dancing. Many that remember him claimed he had a reputation throughout Philadelphia and was considered the best dancer in the Northeast.

Eddie, two years younger, an inch taller, and a few pounds

Legs Diamond.

heavier, had fire-red hair and direct, unflinching dark brown eyes. An expert with a knife and accustomed to violence, he was respected among the young toughs of Philadelphia. At thirteen, he was a vicious sandlot brawler and a sneak thief who caused his mother continual trouble. A hookey player like his brother Legs, he spent most of his time gambling in pool halls as a steerer in a neighborhood where whoring was new. Influenced and protected by Legs, there was little that he would not do in pursuit of a fast dollar—including murder. "That Eddie was the worst of the lot and would put a bullet in you as soon as look at you," said a reporter, who covered the New York scene.

In November of 1913 Sara's condition worsened, a bacterial infection and a high fever had set in. Little could be done for her and she died the day before Christmas. After weeks of grieving, her husband packed his meager possessions, gave notice at the factory, and took his two boys to live with relatives in Brooklyn.

At the time, New York City was one of the leading industrial and commercial centers in the nation. Its skyscrapers, banks, factories, brownstones, and bridges gave it a complexion like that of no other city in the world. Its size alone could easily swallow Philadelphia, and this impressed the Diamonds. New York also had more crime than any other city on the Atlantic coast. In those days, the New York City police were armed with Smith and Wesson revolvers and they patrolled in pairs. In the very tough neighborhoods, seldom was there a policeman to be found.

As far back as the 1880s large gangs, such as the Whyos, dominated lower Manhattan and were living proof of the lawlessness of the late nineteenth century. Acceptance into the Whyos was contingent upon the prospective members committing murder or mayhem. Other contemporary gangs were just as deadly and bold. Crimes such as robbery, even in the daytime were quite common as described in the following case:

> Six of the Daybreak boys in rowboats attacked three boys in a small sloop in New York harbor, just off the Bowery. The boys were beaten, robbed, and thrown into the river and the six thugs

Four members of Legs Diamond's gang in custody of the State Police, spring 1930. Left to right: Jimmy Hart, Tony Fusco, Jimmy Dalton, Paul Quattrochi.

then sailed their boat up the East River, later selling it to a junkman.

Gangs of toughs roamed the Five Points section, the river dens, and the Bowery. The *Police Gazette* reported that along Water Street and in its vicinity one found oneself in the midst of "the lowest dives and most squalid places that ever answered to the name of home." Out of such places came the gangs that acted as clubs for up and coming criminals. Herbert Asbury, the noted authority on early New York City crime, said of the Dusters:

> While they never were such fighters as the Eastmans, the Five Pointers, and the Gophers, they were a rare collection of thugs and much of their reputation was deserved. Perhaps ninety per cent of the Dusters were cocaine addicts and when under the influence of drugs were very dangerous.

The Dusters were already in their decline when Jack and Eddie Diamond arrived, and the gang was finally smashed by the police in 1916. From 1917–1919 competition, between the obstreperous Johnny Spanish and the youthful sneak thief Nathan Kaplan, alias "Kid Dropper," for the control of the Duster

23

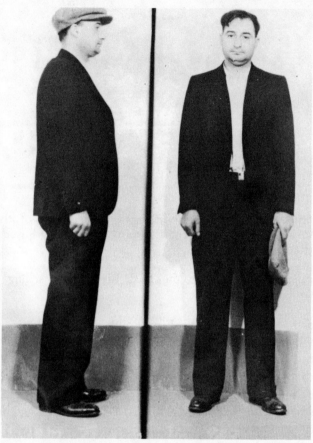

Garry Saccio, Diamond's tough bodyguard.

territory resulted in the shooting of the former. Dropper was
now in charge and even looked the part:

> He appeared along Broadway and throughout the East Side in a
> belted check suit of extreme cut, narrow pointed shoes, and shirts
> and neckties of weird design and color combination, while his
> pudgy face, partly gray from his long imprisonment, was sur-
> rounded by a stylish derby pulled rakishly over one eye.

Kid Dropper became "king of the East Side racketeers," and
in due time was challenged by an up and coming thug named
Jacob "Little Augie" Orgenstein. During the struggle between
the two Orgenstein asked Diamond for help. Legs managed

to buy the services of Louis Kushner, a half-witted truck driver, who was being blackmailed by Dropper for beating a garment worker. On the broiling hot summer day of August 18, 1923, Kushner fired three bullets into Dropper's body killing him instantly, right under the noses of more than fifty New York City policemen who were protecting the criminal. That summer New York's underworld was left without a leader and Jack "Legs" Diamond moved in. And many familiar with the situation believed a conniving Diamond had planned everything for his own takeover.

Group of suspects seized (for questioning) near Diamond's estate by the State Police, September 1930.

Diamond had assembled quite a criminal record, as depicted on page 27, since arriving from Philadelphia. He was arrested in 1914 for breaking into a New York jewelry store and was sent to the New York City Reformatory where he spent a year. Within a few months, of his release, he committed six burglaries and was on the way to a successful criminal career until he was drafted into the army in 1918.

Legs Diamond. New York City Police Department photo.

STATE OF NEW YORK
DEPARTMENT OF CORRECTION

* This is an incomplete record and does not include several arrests made in Catskill, N. Y.

CRIMINAL RECORD   Alias
Jack "Legs" Diamond   "Legs" Schiffer, John Thomas
                                              Diamond, John Hart, John Higgins

2/4/14	As John Diamond; Brooklyn, N.Y.; Burglary; Officer Schlidge, Traffic B.
2/15/14	N.Y.C. Reformatory; Judge Dike.
2/15/14	Sentenced and received 7/26/15 (from N.Y.C. Reformatory); N.Y. County Penitentiary as John Diamond K29596 (Kings Co.) Indefinite Term; Unlawful Entry; Judge Dike.
5/12/16	As John Diamond, N.Y.C.; Assault and Robbery; Officer Duffy, 18th Precinct.
5/12/16	Discharged, Magistrate McQuade.
5/31/16	As John Diamond; N.Y.C.; Grand Larceny; Officer Anderson, 2nd Precinct.
5/31/16	Discharged; Magistrate Murphy.
7/5/16	As John Diamond; N.Y.C.; Assault 3rd, Officer Murphy.
7/14/16	Acquitted; Special Sessions.
3/13/18	As John Diamond; N.Y.C.; Attempted Robbery; Officer Duffy, 23rd Precinct.
3/21/18	Dismissed.
4/16/18	As John Diamond; N.Y.C.; Attempted Robbery, Grand Larceny; Officer Ryan.
5/1/18	Dismissed; Judge MulQueen.
3/24/19	As John Diamond, #6376; U.S. Disciplinary Barracks, Governors Island, N.Y.; From Fort Jay, Escape, Desertion, Larceny, 5 years.
7/7/19	As John T. Diamond, #17513, received at Disciplinary Barracks Fort Leavenworth, Kansas from Governors Island; Sentence 5 years (Violation 95-98, Dept. of Justice.)
6/1/21	As John Diamond; N.Y.C.; Grand Larceny; Officer Flood.
6/2/21	Discharged; Magistrate Ten Eyck nd Court.
10/27/21	As John Hart; N.Y.C.; Assault and Robbery; Detective Moek, 31DD.
10/31/21	Discharged; Magistrate Brough.
11/18/21	As John Diamond; N.Y.C.; Burglary; Detective Corcoran, 16DD.
11/19/21	Discharged; Judge Mancuso.
4/16/22	As John Higgins; N.Y.C.; Material Witness; Detective Boyle, 38DD.
4/17/22	Not held by District Attorney.
11/16/23	As John Diamond; Cliffside, New Jersey; fugitive from justice, N.Y.C.; Delivered to N.Y.C. Police Detective Hayden, MOD.
11/28/23	As John Diamond; N.Y.C.; Robbery; Officer Hastings, MOD.
3/25/24	Discharged; Judge Olvany, General Sessions.
6/12/24	As John Diamond; N.Y.C.; Robbery; Officer Kelly, 14th Squad.

6/14/24	Discharged; Magistrate Oberwager, 12th Court.
1/7/25	As John Diamond; N.Y.C.; Revolver; Officer Moore, 13th Div.
3/28/26	Bail discharged; Judge Koenig.
8/12/25	As John Diamond; Bronx County; Homicide; Officer Sullivan, 18th Squad.
8/18/25	Discharged; Magistrate Vitale, 6th Court.
12/29/26	As John Diamond; N.Y.C.; Felonious Assault; Detective Walsh, MOD.
12/29/26	Discharged; Magistrate Glatzmeyer.
7/9/27	As John Diamond, Mt. Vernon, N.Y.; Smuggling, Narcotics, arrested by Federal Narcotics Agents and Local Police (No Disposition from Federal Authorities).
10/15/27	As John Diamond; N.Y.C.; Homicide; Officer Conway.
12/20/27	Discharged; Magistrate McCreary, Homicide Court.
2/2/28	As John Diamond; N.Y.C.; Homicide; Officer Coons.
2/3/28	Discharged; Magistrate Corrigan.
5/20/29	As John Diamond; N.Y.C.; Homicide; Detective Ferguson, 9th squad.
5/23/29	Discharged; Magistrate McCreary, Homicide Court.
3/10/30	As Jack Diamond, B33628; Arrested Manhattan; Homicide; Sgt. Donnelly.
3/21/30	Discharged; Judge Levine, General Sessions.
7/15/30	As John Diamond; Arrested Manhattan; Fugitive from Justice, Robbery; Newark, N.J.; Detectives McHale and Wilson, MOD.
9/22/30	As John Diamond, #103415; Arrested Philadelphia, Pennsylvania; Suspicious Character.
10/12/30	Shot and wounded, Hotel Monticello, N.Y.C.
4/21/31	As John T. Diamond, arrested Catskill, N.Y.; Assault 2nd; Arrested by Sheriff Every, Undersheriff Ferris, and Trooper Hillfrank.
4/27/31	Shot by an unknown assailant at Aratoga Inn, Acra, Greene County, Taken to Albany Hospital.

"Diamond's army experience at Fort Dix was the worst thing that ever happened to him. He was always fighting with someone and had a couple of teeth knocked down his throat," said Phillip Thomas, a close acquaintance who knew him well. "I was just sick of it, the whole God damn thing, I just had to get out," Diamond would often tell his friends. Frustrated and harrassed, he decided to make a break for it. Armed with a .45 caliber pistol and carrying a sack of flare guns that he intended to sell to a fence, he managed to get by the main gate but was caught a half mile down the main road. In struggling to get away, he struck a sergeant with an iron bar and injured two other soldiers. Charged with desertion, in addition to several other crimes, he was sentenced to Fort Jay and then to Governor's Island in New York City. An attempt to escape here resulted in a sentence of from three to five years at hard labor at the Federal Penitentiary at Fort Leavenworth, Kansas. "No matter what happens they'll never make me serve the full sentence," he said prophetically as they took him away, and he would later receive help from a most unexpected source. In the Spring of 1921 the newly elected President of the United States, Warren G. Harding, in a goodwill gesture, pardoned more than two dozen prisoners in federal penitentiaries, and Legs Diamond's name was the first on the list.

Criminals and bootleggers being transported to prison—stopover at Albany Fall, 1930.

A much wiser Legs Diamond vowed never to be imprisoned again and returned to a Manhattan affected by a postwar economic decline. The stock market had dropped while a high American tariff on European goods and a buyer's strike against high retail prices aggravated the situation. Nationally there were almost three and a half million Americans out of work and almost nine thousand businesses had failed.

Jack and Eddie though, were in a line of work that was hardly affected by the economic malaise. As burglars and robbers they did rather well, breaking and entering a clothing store in the East Thirties, a pawnshop on lower Broadway, or hijacking a truckload of furs on Delancey Street.

Furs always attracted Jack and the police believed that he was responsible for taking a half dozen trucks loaded with this valuable commodity and for burglarizing many fur warehouses.

Capt. Ralph Michelle of the New York City Police Department demonstrates the use of the Thompson submachine gun.

On one Saturday morning in February 1928, two dozen uniformed police officers accompanied by five detectives raided the Paramount Building at Broadway and 42nd Street. Breaking down the main door with fire axes, they rushed in taking the elevator to the fourteenth floor where the Kenton Importing Company was located. With guns drawn and billie clubs raised, they broke through the office door shouting, "Get your hands up or we'll blow your brains out." Caught red-handed with more than $20,000 of hot furs were Eddie and Jack Diamond and fourteen of their associates. Police detectives later said that this was the gang that had shot and killed a watchman during the attempted burglary of the Herman Gabbe and Brothers Fur Company on West 22nd Street. It was also said that this was the gang that had been intimidating fur manufacturers, in Manhattan and Newark, and forcing them to buy hot furs. "You will never make the charges stick on the Diamonds," said famous detective Johnny Broderick, who led the raid. "Frankly, I think those crooks could squeeze their way out of anything. That Diamond will have the best lawyers on his side within a matter of hours, you just wait and see." Broderick was right

Rare lineup photo. Left to right: Eddie Diamond, Legs Diamond, Fatty Walsh, and Lucky Luciano.

and the case never came to trial. The Diamonds were free within twenty-four hours of their arrest.

Undeterred by police harassment, Legs and Eddie plunged deeper into crime. Stealing cars was a pastime of Eddie's, who was usually quite close to Legs most of the time. He had mastered the technique of picking car door locks and switching ignition wires. Packards, Cadillacs, and Pierce Arrows were his favorites because they were big, powerful, and could outrun police vehicles. Once stolen, these cars were taken to a garage in Brooklyn where Eddie altered the serial numbers and made counterfeit registrations. Later, they were sold in New Jersey for a fraction of their cost.

Desperate for the big money, the Diamonds robbed a mail truck with $100,000 worth of cash and securities, making a clean getaway despite a hail of bullets by pursuing police officers. Detectives later picked up two smalltime thugs named Eddie Doyle and John Montforte, who promptly implicated Jack and

Kiki Roberts, spring 1930.

Eddie. But without hard evidence or witnesses the suspects were released.

On the day they left court Babe Pioli, one of Legs' more brutal henchman, shot and killed Bill Brennan, the prize fighter, in his Tijuana nightclub on the west side. Brennan, a top-notch fighter who had faced Jack Dempsey and Luis Firpo, owed Diamond $2,500 on a load of hijacked whiskey. The tough fighter was short on funds and asked for a delay but the thick-headed Pioli, acting on his own, shot the fighter to death. He was caught the same night and after a speedy trial was sent to Sing Sing. Paroled after three years, he would end up murdering his own brother because he refused to pay him a half dollar. For this, he was sent to the electric chair.

Legs Diamond hides his face from a photographer who got into his room at the Bellview Hospital October 26, 1927. He is surrounded by the District Attorney, his staff, and the police.

With the return of prosperity to the city Jack spent his money freely, purchasing a new car and a small bungalow in Cliffside Park, New Jersey. The hustle and bustle of a rejuvenated economy was evident everywhere. The country was riding the crest of the Republican prosperity and the stock market continually rose upward. The demand for hundreds of new products created many jobs. Forecasters predicted the country

33

would have an unparalleled growth and a bountiful future.

The night spots boomed despite the fact that prohibition had been in effect for more than three years. New York City was probably the wettest city in the nation with 5,000 speak-easies scattered throughout its five boroughs. The police usually looked the other way and the failure to enforce the Volstead Law was so obvious that in several cases federal agents openly sold liquor in the speakeasies.

The respectable restaurants and cabarets gave way to these nightclubs and Broadway took on a new atmosphere. Legitimate

Eddie Diamond.

operators were run out of the city simply because they did not make the right deal with the gangsters or pay off the police and politicians. By the mid-twenties all the better known clubs and restaurants were dominated by the big time criminals and business was booming. Profits were big and competition among the clubs was keen. Prices were high at such places and the prospective customer was charged "$1 for two Camel cigarettes in a special package; $6 for a rag doll; $4.50 for Four Roses, as a boutonniere; $1 for a paper gardenia; $2 for a pitcher of water; $10 for a pint of whiskey and $1 for a small bottle of White Rock." The operating and overhead expenses were usually great enough to keep the prices very high. Famed nightclub operator, Sherman Billingsley, who was the first man to put a canopy out in front of a speakeasy, said of his own nightclub operation:

> We can seat about 300 people. There are nearly two hundred employees. That includes 45 waiters, 12 captains, 10 bartenders, 15 musicians, 10 in the concessions, 50 in the kitchen, 8 in the accounting department, 5 porters, 8 bus boys, 5 bar boys, 2 inside door men and 2 outside. . . . It costs as much to feed the help as it does the customers.

Most nightclubs required some form of membership by someone connected with the establishment and that someone could receive a gratuity if the prospect was accepted as a member of the club. Membership cards were given, and the name and address of the new member were entered in registry books.

Nightclubs became the abode of the gangster, the curious, the alcoholic, the big-time spender, and the visitor to the big city. The clubs flourished despite the exorbitant prices, crushing crowds, and loud noise. Police raids were frequent, even against the popular clubs like Club Chantee, Duffey's Tavern, the Lido, and the Montmarte. Texas Guinan's Del Fey Club was very popular with the theatrical crowd and their admirers and was considered to be the most successful of the Broadway night spots. But like the others, it was suspected of distributing illegal booze in large quantities to its customers. Prohibition officers alerted by a tip, observed the many tipsy guests leaving the club and were sure whiskey was being smuggled into the club

Marvin Parks, Diamond's pilot, poses with his Curtis J-5 plane.

right under their noses. But how? In November 1925, agents set up a daily watch on a barber shop next door to the club, that the club's management had rented from 10:00 p.m. to dawn. During these hours a supply of whiskey in pint flasks and quart bottles of champagne were pushed through a small space separating the two establishments by a Del Fey Club employee locked inside the barber shop. When a waiter at the club received an order for a bottle or a flask, he simply tapped on the wall of the barbershop and the much desired liquid appeared through a hole in the wall. Everything worked well until officers noticed Abe Attell, a former prizefighter, who was

Jack and Alice, November 1930.

a friend of Diamond and Arnold Rothstein deliver a suspicious package to the barber shop, that had been closed for several hours. A raid followed that netted Attell, the Del Rey Club employee, a barber shop full of booze and the discovery of a loose brick that separated the Club and the barbershop.

Dance halls also dotted the White Way and attracted many. For the price of a ticket, which varied from one to five dollars, you could find a partner or dance with a partner you brought along. Pretty ex-typists and waitresses worked evenings as hostesses. For a dollar you got twelve dance tickets in such cheaper houses as the Balconades, on Columbus Avenue and 66th Street, and the Dreamland Academy, at 120 west 125th Street. Lonely ladies sought out the Roseland on Broadway and the hosts the establishment offered, while the Irish met at the New Mayo Ballrooms. The dancehalls attracted those who could not always afford nightclubs, especially up-and-coming gangsters like Jack and Eddie Diamond.

Jack frequented several of the dancehalls regularly during his first few years in the city, especially favoring the Clover Gardens, at Grand Central Palace, and the New Mayo Ballrooms. When it came to the blackbottom or the Charleston he always cleared the floor, gathering about him a large group of admiring females.

If there was anything that he wanted most, it was to improve his social status and to be accepted into respectable society. To this end you could find him in any number of nightclubs, where New York's upper crust could be found. He strutted into a club wearing his flashy blue suit and checked cap, smoking a corked-tip cigarette, smiling at everyone. Jack liked the adulation, the stares, and the autograph seekers. He liked the tough guy syndrome of tough talking, fearlessness, imperviousness to bullets, and appealing to women. "That Diamond liked to hear himself talk, he liked to impress people, and play bigshot," commented Al Gruber, a bartender at the Kenmore Hotel. "He was always smiling, shaking hands, and sometimes he would crack a dirty joke or two. But above all, he really was friendly and people liked him," recalled another bartender. What the bar patrons did not see was a tough, unscrupulous, and cold-blooded gangster, who would shoot a competitor right between the eyes

Police Chief George Klein.

without any remorse whatsoever. Remember, the press called him "cobra" while his enemies referred to him as "a snake" and "a cold-blooded killer."

By the mid-1920s Jack "Legs" Diamond, nearing his twenty-eighth birthday, had a taste for money and good times, something he did not want to relinquish. He had gone through several new cars, owned a new house, bought his suits in the most exclusive clothing stores in Manhattan, and drank the best

Arnold Rothstein.

Scotch and Canadian whiskey. He numbered among his associates every aspiring thug in the city, many corrupt cops and local politicians, and the all-powerful Arnold Rothstein. As successor to the late Nathan "Kid" Dropper, Diamond put together a gang specializing in robberies, hijacking, and bootlegging. The membership in this newly formed group included Charles "Lucky" Luciano, Arthur "Dutch Schultz" Fleggenheimer, and jewel thief Eugene Moran. This gang of up and coming racketeers and bootleggers had all the money and contacts necessary to carry out big operations. It proved that Diamond had financially succeeded on his own, with an organization apart from

Jack "Legs" Diamond. 1929 State Police photo.

anything Rothstein controlled. But he could not control the group or get along with the "wops," as he called them. There were times when he cursed them and their pals, and was remembered to have on one occasion pointed his gun at a group of them gathered together to talk business. He would constantly say to Eddie, "You just can't trust that Luciano or his friends Willie Moretti and Longie Zwillman, who run things in Jersey." Arguments over the division of the loot were a constant problem and the gangsters faced each other over gun barrels many times. Luciano gave Diamond most of the trouble with his own killers and organization. He could get along with just about anyone, especially if the price was right. Diamond, on the other hand, resorted to cheating his partners. And although there were several get-togethers at Diamond's Acra estate and some big profits on a few hijacking jobs, the group dissolved in the summer of 1928.

It was at this time that the fortunes of Jack and Eddie Diamond were to take an upward turn. By Christmas Eve 1925, they and several other gangsters, with clever backing from Arnold Rothstein, came to dominate the labor situation in New York City. In fact, many of gangdom's big names got their start in labor. Tough and crude Sam Parks, the six-foot-three-inch head of the 4,000 member Housesmiths, Bridgemen, and Structural Workers Union, was a pioneer in extortion, blackmail, strongarm tactics, and other criminal activity. Parks, many believe, brought the huge George A. Fuller Construction Company to its knees in 1900 with his assorted criminal acts. It was slim and gaunt Larry Fay who set up Texas Guinan at the Del Fey Club and who organized New York City's 40,000 taxi drivers. The always dangerous Jacob "Gurrah" Shapiro and the arch criminal Louis Buchalter ran a group called the East Side Industrialists, that represented unions numbering over 200,000 members. It was Buchalter who directed the notorious Murder Incorporated, that hired out killers to the underworld.

By the time of the garment industries strike of 1926, the directorates of conflict were no simple matter of labor versus management.

Unions fought unions. Factions within the same union fought each other. Employers found themselves on opposite sides of the battle. In some locals right wing fought left wing. In others two left wing factions fought each other. One union might join an employer to fight a second local. And an employer might give aid to a local that the shop on the floor below was trying to destroy.

Behind most of the squabbling, head breaking, and power plays was the ominous figure of Arnold Rothstein. Known as "King of the Roaring Twenties," "The Brain," and "King of the Gamblers," Rothstein during the twenties had his hand in any criminal activity where there was a large profit to be made. His success in crime enabled him to bankroll other criminals and finance many shady transactions. He was born in 1882, in New York City, the second son of poor Russian Jewish parents. At age three, he had already revealed certain criminal proclivities when he tried to kill his older brother Harry with a knife. The rivalry continued between the two for many years until at age sixteen he dropped out of school and set out on his own. Obsessed with an uncontrollable urge to cheat and to take a chance, he turned to gambling and to playing the percentages. He soon saw a quick way to earn a fast buck by making loans to players in crap games, with the borrower having to return six dollars for every five he borrowed. Money lending became one of Rothstein's big operations and eventually he became the underworld's biggest moneylender. But the racket that put him into the bigtime was the theft of valuable securities from Wall Street brokerage houses. Rothstein sent his mobsters into the streets to take the Liberty Bonds right from the hands of messenger boys. In some cases, these messenger boys were paid out and gladly gave up the bonds. Before long, millions of dollars worth of bonds were stolen and the police in desperation, and after a tip, went after Jules W. Arnstein, husband of Broadway star Fanny Brice and known to the theatrical world as Nicky Arnstein. Rothstein had framed Arnstein and got away with one of the biggest thefts of the century.

It was also Rothstein who was behind the 1919 World Series fix involving eight players of the Chicago Black Sox, that evoked the classic plea of the American boy to his hero, "Say it ain't so, Joe." Arnold Rothstein had almost destroyed professional baseball, yet had again got away with a classic crime.

The labor-management relations of the period were ready made for Rothstein to exploit. The Jewish dominated unions needed someone to act for them and they picked Rothstein only because they trusted his pious and honest father, Abraham. Little did they know that Arnold, for the right price, would gladly do them in. Being in the position of serving both labor and management brought Rothstein untold success and many new contacts. During the 1926 garment strike one prominent labor leader charged that Rothstein, who was a mediator during the trouble, used his influence with Mayor Walker's office to protect the communists.

Rothstein's power continued to grow. He engineered the importation of huge amounts of whiskey and drugs into the country and corrupted a host of public officials in the process. He owned shares in many nightclubs and businesses, and was on intimate terms with influential politicians and police officials. In spite of a deepseated compulsion as a gambler, he did well in most of his enterprises and had amassed a small fortune for himself. He had the money, the hired thugs, and the right contacts to arrange just about anything for a price. His wife, Carolyn, characterized her husband as being,

> more likely to have inside knowledge of the latest devices for cheating; the latest scheme for making bets safe in any branch of sports, than any other person in the country. As the biggest figure, as the unique figure in his particular line of endeavor, he was the repository of secrets, the court of last resort.

Legs Diamond became Rothstein's official bodyguard, consultant on drugs and whiskey, and hit man. Rothstein, in turn, protected Diamond from the authorities and financed many of his gang's operations. As Rothstein's power and operations grew in scope he came to rely more on Legs who, in turn, grabbed a bigger share of Rothstein's profits for himself. Legs guaranteed the security of Rothstein's fifty and one-hundred-thousand-dollar card games and when a gambler was found floating in the Hudson River, it was a good guess that Diamond had escorted him home.

2

Assault on a City

Supplying bootleg booze was one of the biggest businesses in the country. Al Capone was quick to sum up his operation by saying, "I make my money by supplying a public demand. If I break the law my customers, who number hundreds of the best people in Chicago, are as guilty as I am." Accused of supplying New York City's speakeasies and reacting to being labled public enemy number one, Dutch Schultz said, "I never did anything to deserve that, unless it was to supply good beer to people who wanted it."

At the height of prohibition the thousands of speakeasies in New York City operated so openly, that they proved to be a serious problem for the 180 prohibition agents assigned to put them out of business. By 1925 at least a dozen big-time gangsters and a multitude of small alky brewers were distributing their stuff throughout New York's five boroughs, while most of the police looked the other way.

Enforcing the Eighteenth Amendment was more of a task than many had originally believed. The 1,500 agents of the Prohibition Bureau and the law enforcement officers throughout the country who cooperated with them struck at stills, roadhouses, delicatessens, night spots, farms, or wherever illicit alcohol was reported or suspected. In 1926 alone, the Commissioners for the Internal Revenue Service reported that prohibition agents had made 58,391 arrests, seized 5,935 automobiles and 187 boats, and that 41,544 individuals had been convicted. Within four years 282,122 stills were seized and 61,383 individuals convicted. Detection and apprehension were always front-page news, with some agents attracting as much attention as the gangsters. Using disguises to snare their quarry, famous agents Izzy Einstein and Moe Smith passed as mechanics, rabbis, and gravediggers in their hunt for bootleggers. In April of 1925, they outraged many of their fellow Jews by seizing $4,000 worth of sacramental wine from a store in Brooklyn. The booze, however, poured into the country from Europe, Mexico, and Canada in such quantities that the authorities could not handle it. The Border Patrol estimated that there were about 550 roads and many trails from Canada, most of them unpatrolled. The figures for Mexico were four times as high.

Although undermanned, the Border Patrol and the Coast Guard made it hot for the smugglers, especially those who carried their booze on converted yachts, tramp steamers, and large fishing schooners. A typical haul consisted of between 3,000 and 4,000 cases, carried by a large ship which anchored beyond the three mile limit and passed the cargo to small speed boats whose skippers ultimately took the chances. Such operations were usually well conceived, and magazine accounts read not unlike the popular adventure fiction of the day:

> Bootleggers are turning more to radio as their best means of communication. One instance was the fake distress messages that reported a ship sinking in the Atlantic thirty miles off Barnegat, New Jersey. The message came weakly, hesitantly, as if exhausted or from an inexperienced sender. Twenty boats rushed to the spot, among them were three coast guard cutters, two destroyers and a seaplane. They found no ship in distress. . . . The rum runner then had come ashore unmolested.

In New York City the demand for alcohol far exceeded the supply and at first there was enough business for everyone. One of the biggest bootleggers was "Big Bill" Dwyer, who directed his operations from two luxurious Manhattan offices. Dwyer already had controlling interests in nightclubs, gambling casinos, and racetracks throughout the northeast. He gained credit for bringing ice hockey to New York City and the Brooklyn Dodgers football club to Brooklyn. He earned the sobriquet "Big" from the vastness of his operations, not from his size. Known both to the police and the press, he was described as "of average height, blond, soft-spoken, his face round and ruddy, a conservative dresser . . ." A good organizer with a sound head for figures, he had many friends in crime, among them Frank Costello, who organized the rum-running operations and was the contact man for the payoffs. It was Costello who bribed Coast Guard crews, prohibition agents, politicians, and who equipped the speedboats with Liberty engines. Needless to say, Dwyer became immensely wealthy and successful, so much so that a small time runner had to pay him two dollars a case to get his rum in the New York area. Preferring to compromise rather than to fight the competition, he lasted longer than most of his kind.

One of his toughest competitors was English born Owney Madden, the most durable bootlegger of them all. By age twenty-three, he had already killed five men and was among the best shots in Manhattan. His headquarters at the Winona Club in Manhattan was equipped with an arsenal that contained pistols, shotguns, bombs, and burglar tools. Described by the police as "crafty and cruel," he never did an honest day's work in his life, spending his time in crime or combat with enemy

Aratoga Inn, Cairo, New York.

gangs. He was in prison from 1919 to 1923 for murdering the former suitor of his girlfriend, and missed being convicted in several other murders only because the witnesses conveniently vanished. A short time after his release from prison, he was arrested with five others for possession of $25,000 in liquor stolen from the home of wealthy Stockbridge, Massachusetts, broker James Malloy. Claiming in his defense that he was an innocent hitchhiker, "who had begged for a ride on the truck that he did not know was full of hot booze," was sufficient to get the charges dismissed. His tough countenance and notorious reputation were not enough to scare away competitors who muscled in on his and "Big Bill" Dwyer's bootleg empires.

Another up-and-coming bootlegger was Irving Wexler, alias Waxey Gordon, who was a protege of the Benny Fein gang, of labor racketeering fame. By 1925, Gordon had established a large whiskey operation that did more than $200,000 in business a month, mainly by running in booze from the Canadian sea lanes. Emory R. Buckner, the aggressive United States Attorney for the Southern District, eventually raided Gordon's headquarters at the Knickberbocker Building, closing down his operations permanently. Putting Gordon out of business, though, only opened up opportunities for other rum runners.

Jack and Eddie Diamond were quick to learn the tricks of the trade. Acting on their own and for Arnold Rothstein, they were soon rolling in greenbacks. The Diamonds excelled particularly at hijacking booze from Dwyer's trucks, and this irked the Irishman because he went through so much trouble to get the stuff. With their accomplice Vannie Higgins, the Diamond boys stocked several garages and warehouses in Brooklyn with hot booze and awaited eager buyers. In the meantime, Dwyer and Madden passed the word that anyone caught with their booze would get a bellyful of lead. Referring to Legs in a loud booming voice Big Bill said, "he was nothing but a river pirate come to New York City," and promised "that no good son-of-bitch will get his, if it's the last thing I do."

On a cool October afternoon in 1924, Legs was driving his Dodge sedan on Fifth Avenue on his way to the Bronx. Suddenly, a big black limousine pulled along side with the long barrel of a shotgun sticking from the passenger side. Two blasts later and Legs Diamond had his first taste of battle. Fortunately most of the pellets went into the car, with a few striking him in the left side of the head and in his left foot. Stepping on the accelerator, he managed to drive to Mount Sinai Hospital, where he received emergency treatment. When asked by the police about the shooting, he said, "I ain't done nothing wrong. I dunno a thing about it, maybe they got the wrong guy." Later on he quietly confided to his new girlfriend Kiki, "I won't take any more chances traveling alone. From now on I will be with Eddie or one of the boys. There will be some artillery in the car. Maybe I ought to get one of those big bullet-proof jobs like Johnny Torrio has in Chicago."

Giving matters time to cool off, he devoted more attention to his speakeasies in the Bronx and Manhattan. Almost all gangsters in New York City had interests in speakeasies that varied in type and size. The most numerous were the barrooms, fully equipped with foot rail, cuspidors, and a back room, "where the goods were delivered." A second type was the grill, open only to known regulars, where crooners, torch singers, or quartets could be found performing before a busy bar. Another common type was the dingy room, located in a brownstone basement, where whiskey was served at tables, the lights were kept low, and everyone spoke softly. Women preferred this type of place above all. They also liked the so-called "second-floor speakeasy," that had its entrance in a basement. Here one found a table d' hote, possibly a jazz band, and a bright, highly obtrusive decor. The grandest and most spectacular of them all was the mansion speakeasy, à la *The Great Gatsby,* where dancehalls, bars, ping-pong, backgammon rooms, and bands could be found. Champagne was twenty-five dollars a quart, cocktails were a dollar each, and admission was through a friend. An electrical system at the main door, triggered by a guard's finger on a buzzer, warned the patrons of an unscheduled police visit giving them time to disappear into the woods.

The least desirable place to get the booze was the cat joint or clip joint, although technically a speakeasy it served the real purpose of bilking the patron of his money. The victims were usually steered to these places by taxi drivers. Once in, they were greeted by peroxide blondes, jazz bands, and served watered-down whiskey and fake champagne. When the patron had had enough, he was usually kicked out into the street by burly bouncers. Any objections could result in a trip to the hospital.

At the time a committee, known as the "Committee of Fourteen," conducted an investigation of 373 nightclubs and speakeasies. They found that:

Of these, 52 are believed to be respectable. From the remaining 321 there are reports on 806 hostesses and other women employees, of whom 487 acknowledged that they were prostitutes. In addition, there are reports on 418 other prostitutes who were permitted to

Charles Entratta.

solicit customers and 260 procurers, connected with the business of commercialized prostitution, who were found in these clubs.

Diamond's most successful speakeasy was the Hotsy Totsy Club, a very popular place located on the second floor at 1721 Broadway, between 54th and 55th streets. Although it consisted of a large hardwood dancefloor, an adjoining bar that had a huge mirror for a backdrop, and a dining area with thirty tables and chairs, it was not ostentatious by any standard. Just off the bar was a large storage closet, full of cases of illicit whiskey. Business was always good with the weekends bringing in crushing crowds including many out of town visitors. Henry Boechel, a front man, was listed as the club's owner and Charles Entratta, alias Charlie Green, was Diamond's partner in this operation as well as in several other illegal activities. Entratta, who had a large home on Trenton Avenue in Long Beach, Long Island, was part owner of the Superior Paper Products Company and the J. Winkenfeld Bottling Works, both in Long Island City. It was widely rumored at the time that Entratta and Diamond used the bottling works to make illegal beer for the New York City area. The rumor mongers were probably correct, for some observers claimed that trucks came and went from the plant taking some four hundred cases of beer a day to Manhattan's best bars and nightspots.

As Jack and Eddie prospered the police and politicians extracted larger payoffs, a common occurrence during prohibition. Every week, almost on schedule, a neat, well-dressed member of New York's finest visited the Hotsy Totsy Club for his payoff. Occasionally, a representative of Tammany Hall asked the Diamonds for a contribution to the Democratic party. This was mainly because the Diamonds were linked to Rothstein and Rothstein was linked to the Democrats.

At the time there was a stiff battle for control of Tammany Hall between George Olvaney, the boss in 1925, and his challengers, Albert Marinelli and Jimmy Hines. Olvaney had succeeded the brilliant Charles W. Murphy, whom Mayor Jimmy Walker once called "the brains of Tammany Hall," but he could not keep power. Olvaney and Tammany were still calling the shots in 1925 and still keeping the gangsters in check. In ex-

changing favors for gangster money, the gangsters soon handed
out the favors and the politicians became the favor seekers.
Arnold Rothstein became the power broker between Tammany
and the gangsters, and Legs Diamond soon found himself involved in the corrupt politics of the day. The list of gangster
bigshots that received something from City Hall was big enough
to include almost every hoodlum in the city. From 1927–1932,
New York City was an excellent example of a breakdown in
democratic government that was probably unparalleled in politics
up to that time. Corruption became so widespread that Major
Maurice Campbell, Prohibition Administrator for the metro-

Prohibition agents look over haul of booze taken in raid in downtown Manhattan, spring 1928.

politan district, believed that prohibition could not be enforced chiefly because of politics. His own experience had been that,

> prohibition enforcement is honeycombed with political trickery, insincerity, and corruption radiating from Washington and every state, city, and town in the United States. Of course, there seeps back into the prohibition system corruption and paralysis from every criminal source possible.

Major Campbell's words stung the politicians, who were painted in the mass media as collaborators with the gangsters in defying the prohibition law. He even went so far as to declare to President Herbert Hoover that he had documentary evidence showing that Assistant Secretary of the Treasury, Seymour Lowman was "insincere in enforcing the Volstead Act and was derelict in his duty." Several years later Special Investigator Thomas E. Dewey showed through his prosecutions that Tammany Hall was riddled with corrupt politicians, who worked hand in hand with the gangsters. Jimmy Hines, a long time boss of Tammany, would eventually end up in Sing Sing for his criminal association with Dutch Schultz. New York City's jovial, whiskey drinking mayor, Jimmy Walker, a friend of the wets, enforced the prohibition laws only when there was violence, rowdiness or when curfews were blatantly violated. Walker believed that strict enforcement of the three o'clock curfew would reduce the number of speakeasies in the city and curtail crime. In a plea to the Board of Estimate, he stated that at the time his law was put into effect, there was a marked decrease in the number of nightclubs, with a great number of them going out of business. Walker said he was informed that,

> they are increasing in great numbers and that many new ones are opening up. I am told on reliable authority that a lot of them are keeping open until 5 o'clock or even all night with impunity. As I understand the matter, the eradication of night clubs that defy or violate this law is the joint duty of both police and license departments.

Within a few months following Mayor Walker's statement, Police Commissioner Grover Whalen struck hard at the speak-easies and nightclubs, raiding on the average of sixty a night until some six hundred of them were closed down. The establishments owned by Helen Morgan and Texas Guinan were raided several times. On one occasion in December 1927, two dozen prohibition agents and as many police swooped down on Helen Morgan's club breaking up the place and then carried

New York City Police Commissioner Grover Whalen, 1930.

off the furniture. Strangely enough, the Hotsy Totsy Club and other speakeasies owned by the gangster bigshots still were in operation. Many questioned whether Grover Whalen was also on the take. Did the gangster bigshots use the politicians and erase the competition? These and other questions preyed on the minds of many, as control of the illicit trade in whiskey and beer gravitated to a few hands.

As the gangsters competed with one another for prime territory the city became a battleground. Frank Uale (Yale) and Frank Marlowe confronted Al Capone's New York agents and Ciro Terranova. Vincent "mad dog" Coll went out on his own and opposed his former boss Dutch Schultz and his ally Joey Noe. Giusseppi Masseria sent his guns against Salvatore Maranzano in one of the Mafia's first big wars and Owney Madden did his best to get "mad dog" Coll. The metropolitan dailies made exciting reading as machine guns blazed and gangsters bit the dust. What was so common in Chicago, had now come to New York City. On July 1, 1928, Frankie Uale was shot to death in broad daylight in the Bay Ridge section of Brooklyn. A speeding Nash sedan pulled alongside of Uale's new Lincoln coupe and poured one hundred, .45 caliber bullets into him. On April 25, 1931, Joe "the boss" Masseria was shot to death in a Coney Island restaurant. Salvatore Maranzano was shot four times, stabbed six times, and had his throat cut on September 10, 1931, while he sat in his office in the New York Central Building on Park Avenue. In fact, the same day that Marazano fell, some forty Sicilianos joined him in what appeared to be the bloodiest day for organized crime.

As the guns blazed, new and more obstreperous gangsters came into power. Joey Noe, pronounced Noy, and Arthur "Dutch Schultz" Fleggenheimer were prospering in the Bronx and Manhattan. According to Schultz's biographer their operation grew so fast that they did not have enough whiskey and beer to supply the demand. Deals had to be made with such petty hoodlums as Frenchy Dillon and Jay Culhane, who had brewery operations in Manhattan and New Jersey.

One of the Noe-Schultz drops, an underground affair called "the Tins," was so elaborate it was practically a show place. It had disappearing elevators that took empty beer trucks down to a huge loading area and sent them up fully packed and on their way not only to the Bronx outlets but eventually moving as well into Manhattan's upper West Side and down into Yorkville and Harlem.

The small time beer runner hardly stood a chance against these enterprising hoodlums. Joe Rock, a stubborn Irishman, refused to step aside for them, in spite of innumerable threats, and he would pay the full price for his foolishness. He was kidnapped, "beaten, hung up by the thumbs on a meat hook, and then blindfolded with a strip of gauze that had been dipped into a mixture containing the drippings from a gonorrhea infection." When his family got him back, after paying a $35,000 ransom, he was a blind and broken man.

Schultz's ruthlessness, however, did the trick and competing bootleggers were driven out of the Bronx. Almost overnight his organization expanded everywhere gathering to its side a host of triggermen such as Edward Popke, alias "Fats" McCarthy, and Vincent "Mad Dog" Coll. When they pushed into Legs Diamond's territory though, the machine guns blazed.

Diamond had carefully planned to get both Schultz and Noe in an ambush set for October 15, 1928 at 7:00 a.m. outside the Chateau Madrid, on west 54th Street near Sixth Avenue. At the time Schultz was in "Big Bill" Dwyer's office and Noe was outside the nightclub when a big blue Cadillac sped past, with a machine gun blazing away at Noe. Although he was wearing a bullet proof vest, the gangster was hit in the lower part of his chest, his spine, and in his left hand. As he fell, he managed to get off a few shots at his antagonists. The shot up Caddie was later found by police with the corpse of a small time hoodlum and Diamond associate, Louis Weinberg, in the back seat. Noe died a few weeks later and police never found the evidence to pin it on Legs. From this time on Schultz and Diamond were bitter enemies. Insiders in the Schultz organization occasionally heard their boss say, "I have to plug that Diamond or run him into the ground. It has to be done or our operations will be ruined."

Schultz's threats not withstanding, Diamond's career took a swing upward and he became an integral part of New York City's rackets, drug peddling, and bootlegging operations. In

1924, he was already a bodyguard in Arnold Rothstein's organization and played a major role in breaking up a plot against his new employer when he eliminated Chicago's Eugene "Red" McClaughlin, who was planning to kidnap the gambler and hold him for a $100,000 ransom. Chicago newspapers reported that McClaughlin, weighted down with boulders, was found in a ditch in Cook County's Sanitary Canal. This deed made Legs a top Rothstein aide displacing Tom "fatty" Walsh, who had held the job for more than three years.

One of his first big assignments was to supply the muscle in a labor dispute, raging at the time among the painters. Arnold Rothstein was sought as a mediator, by both labor and management, and was able to keep the police in the background while he dealt with the dispute. As soon as he was paid by both

Jacob "Little Augie" Orgenstein.

sides he arranged with the employers to hire "Little Augie" Orgenstein, and for the strikers to hire Louis "Lepke" Buckhalter and Charlie "Gurrah" Shapiro. "Little Augie" was paid $50,000 to do his part, receiving $30,000 in advance.

Jack and Eddie were assigned to protect Orgenstein, who was a target for a half dozen gangs in the city. From his headquarters on Eighth Avenue near Times Square, he ran several small speakeasies and was involved in a number of hijackings. "I'm going to be as big as Rothstein," boasted the shrewd Orgenstein to Legs. "What do you mean big?" answered Legs. "To be big you have to have a lot of dough and contacts. Do you have them?" Turning towards Legs, the stubby little scarfaced gangster countered, "I'll cut you in on half of everything, Rothstein gets nothing." Legs chuckled, "Lets see how you do against the strikers first, then maybe I'll take your offer seriously."

Eddie Diamond could offer his brother little help having gone into hiding from the police. Jack, nervously glancing at his pearl-handled .38 caliber revolver, agreed to protect Orgenstein by himself, even though he knew it was a dangerous job.

On the morning of October 15 Legs and Orgenstein, oblivious to the chill wind, began making their rounds reaching Delancey and Norfolk Streets at about 8:30 p.m. Suddenly three young toughs, who had been standing on the corner of Norfolk Street watching every move Diamond and Orgenstein made, wheeled and started firing at them. Little Augie, their target, took a bullet in his right temple that blew his straw hat some three feet into the air and he died instantly. Jack was hit twice, once in his right side, once in his right lung, and lay bleeding on the sidewalk. Within minutes, a crowd of hundreds gathered around the bloody scene and blocked for several minutes the ambulance attendants from getting through to the stricken gangsters. Rushed to Bellview Hospital in critical condition, he was immediately administered a saline solution and a blood transfusion. His face was ashen, his eyes quivered and stared coldly out into space. A surgeon operated to prevent further complications and removed a large slug from his chest. Within a few days Diamond was on the road to recovery and had escaped the often expected post-operative shock and pneu-

58

monia. This was a remarkable feat at this time because infections were commonplace and antibiotics unknown.

He had suddenly become the center of attention and a noted newspaper personality. The press had waited for days for a picture and caught Jack by surprise on their first encounter. One photographer rushed into his room and Jack, still gun-shy, put a pillow over his face as the flash went off. When confronted by the police and the District Attorney, Jack listened intently to their questions countering, "I can't tell you a thing. I don't know who those dirty bastards were that let us have it. I'll bet you will never find them, no matter what you do." The police continued to pursue leads that eventually led them to believe the shooting resulted from a feud between the remnants of the Kid Dropper gang and Orgenstein. Three weeks before the shooting a member of the Dropper gang had been killed, an innocent bystander slain, and several passersby wounded in a gun battle at Rivington and Forsyth Streets. Some informed observers believed that Jacob "Gurrah" Shapiro, Legs' constant nemesis, had a hand in the shooting. But the mystery was never solved.

Legs' troubles with the police were just beginning. In July 1929 he, once again, hit the front pages of the New York dailies after an incident that took the lives of two petty hoodlums. The trouble began when Peter and William Cassidy, tough waterfront brawlers, and a couple of friends walked into Diamond's Hotsy Totsy Club. Already half drunk, the small group of toughs were boisterous and unruly. Walter Wolgast, a waiter, ordered them to keep quiet or they would get tossed out into the street. Red Cassidy, who was thumping on the bar for service, turned to Wolgast and said, "Drop dead you filthy little worm. This God damn place is nothing but a clip joint." At that moment Simon Walker, Red Cassidy's friend, turned toward Hymie Cohen, the club's manager, and grabbing him by the sleeve uttered, "You four-eyed, fat slob! What the hell is the matter with this place? If we don't get service we will break it into pieces." Walker, a tough ex-convict, who was armed to the teeth with a knife, a blackjack, and two pistols pushed Cohen down on the floor. Diamond and Entratta saw the commotion and rushed toward Walker. "I'm Legs Diamond and

I run this place. If you don't calm down I'll blow your head off."
Walker looked Diamond straight in the eyes and responded,
"You no good bastard, you can't push me around." Before anyone knew what was happening, Legs and his partner drew their
guns and fired point blank into the Cassidys and Walker, who
were approaching menacingly. As the band struck up a lively
tune and the women patrons screamed, the speakeasy became
a shooting gallery. William "Red" Cassidy, 36 years old, was
shot three times in the head, once in the abdomen, and once
in the groin. Simon Walker, 35 years old, his loud friend, received
a half dozen bullets in his torso. Both were very dead when
the police arrived. Peter Cassidy lay dying at the bottom of a
flight of stairs with three bullet holes in him and was taken
to the hospital in critical condition. Guns were found on or
near the deceased men, all of whom had criminal records.

More than fifty people, including employees and patrons,
saw the shootings yet no one would be available to testify
against Legs and Entratta. Through intimidation and murder
every material witness was eliminated. Within six weeks after
the shootings Hymie Cohen, who was held in protective custody
several days by the police, and three waiters were killed in
cold blood. The bullet ridden body of one waiter, Walter
Wolgast of Manhattan, was found July 19, in Bordentown, New
Jersey. A subsequent police investigation showed that the rest
of the victims were killed in New York and dumped in New
Jersey. The remaining witnesses became so terrified that they
had a lapse of memory and the police case against Legs and
Entratta collapsed. At the height of the investigation Police
Commissioner Grover Whalen declared, "Gangdom is in control
of the nightclubs and decent people will shun them if they
want to avoid police attention." The Hotsy Totsy Club shootings,
if they did anything at all, revealed a dreary picture of law
enforcement in New York City. During the first six months of
1929 there were 160 murders, but only thirteen convictions for
homicide. Approximately $2,914,999 worth of property was stolen
and sixty-four percent of the total crimes went unpunished.
Mayor Jimmy Walker vehemently denied the existence of a crime
wave, stating that he was satisfied with the work of the police.
Before long he became a target for the Seabury Commission

Mayor Jimmy Walker on right.

investigators who proved there was a link between crime and public officials.

Under heavy pressure the police continued to harass Jack and Eddie, who spent most of their time hiding in Acra or in their lawyer's office. Eddie quickly buckled under the strain. His complexion turned pale, his frail body became wracked with a constant cough and he was spitting blood. Eddie Diamond had tuberculosis. The best doctors could only advise rest, good food, and a change in climate. It was Salvatore Spitale, Legs' associate in so many illegal activities, who persuaded his gangster pal to purchase an unpretentious two family house in the

Catskill mountain village of Acra, New York, a four and a half hour drive by car from New York City. Eddie's condition worsened at Acra and a short stay at the tuberculosis hospital at Schroon Lake, New York did not bring the expected improvement. As a last alternative, Eddie went to Denver, Colorado hoping the cool mountain air there would bring him relief.

Meanwhile, in New York City, events were moving fast. On November 4, 1928 Arnold Rothstein was shot down. Ten days later he died, in the Polyclinic Hospital, still refusing to name the man who shot him. "Rothstein was probably the most widely known gambler in the United States," blared the front page of the *New York Herald Tribune*. It could have added that he was the biggest big shot in the underworld. His death set off a chain reaction that has not ended even today. But who killed him? He always dealt with killers, even lived among them, though he was of a higher stratum. And he might have,

> feared for his life if, like Benny Rosenthal, he had broken the first commandment of the underworld: Thou shalt not squeal. But he held this commandment in reverence. No, he did not think he was marked for death. Certainly not for failing to pick up his markers.

"The Rothstein murder has raised hell," said Mayor Jimmy Walker and he was right. The politicians and gangsters wanted secrecy and the investigation into the killing became a coverup. George McManus, the gambler friend of Rothstein, was initially charged with the murder and several others were taken into custody as material witnesses. The people's case against McManus however, was too weak for a conviction and the gambler was freed, leaving the search for Rothstein's killer at a standstill. Legs Diamond's role in all of this, though, has hardly been explored thoroughly. According to Rothstein's wife Carolyn, the Diamonds had a powerful hold on her late husband's affairs with Legs getting $30,000 and Eddie $20,000 annually for protection. Carolyn was sure that her husband, up to the moment of his death, never admitted fear or that he had the Diamonds on the payroll for protection. "He salved his conscience, and in his own mind maintained a hold over them by lending them money and then not paying it to them. The causes for his fear became apparent after this." Arnold's life had been

Jack and Alice, fall 1930.

threatened on several occasions. One evening his custom-built Hispano-Suiza limousine was riddled with machine gun bullets, although no one was in the vehicle at the time. On another occasion their home was visited by two rough customers, who threatened to get Arnold. Was Legs Diamond behind all of this?

It was common knowledge, among New York's underworld, that Legs was a victim of a Rothstein doublecross in late 1927. William Mellin, a top narcotics agent, supported this belief when he told a New York newspaper that he arrested Diamond on a narcotics charge after receiving a tip from Rothstein. Always willing to make a deal to avoid prosecution Rothstein agreed with Mellin to set Diamond up at Mount Vernon, where he was sent to sell drugs. The terms of the Mellin-Rothstein deal were supposedly kept strictly secret. In fact to avoid suspicion, Rothstein later put up $15,000 bail to get Diamond out on the street. But Diamond, through the grapevine, heard of the doublecross and vowed to get even. He is the one most likely to have shot his former employer, for a showdown between the two had been coming for a long time. Since Diamond wanted a greater share of the narcotics traffic, he was ready to grab a good piece of Rothstein's empire and to do this he had to eliminate most of his organization.

On March 21, 1930, some fifteen months after Rothstein's death, Newark, New Jersey Deputy Police Chief Frank E. Brex said that there was a feud between the late Rothstein's gang and the Diamond brothers. It was this feud that caused the death of Eugene Moran, Rothstein's top aide, who was once a model for Arrow shirts. Diamond's gangsters caught Moran in downtown Manhattan, shot him several times in the head, then transported the car and his body to the Newark City Dump where both were set afire. Brex said, "Moran was paid $1,000 a week by Rothstein, for bodyguard duties, and was also involved in several large jewelry holdups that netted him more than $30,000." The hot jewels, it was believed, were then sold to Rothstein. On May 15, 1930 his girlfriend, Anna Urbas was strangled and her body thrown into the East River. According to the police, she knew too much—including who took her boyfriend for a one way ride.

Frank Devlin, murdered by Diamond.

The warfare between Diamond's gang and the remnants of Rothstein's organization continued well into 1929. The day after Rothstein was shot Eugene Moran, Frank "Blubber" Devlin, and James Piteo went to Denver, Colorado to ambush Eddie Diamond. Caught in his own car Eddie managed to escape unharmed, although more than a hundred .45 caliber machine gun bullets were fired at him. Moran and Piteo were later caught by the police and after a hearing were released in $15,000 bail each, but promptly fled Denver. Upon hearing of the attempt on Eddie's life Legs promised, "I'll get every one of those bastards and anyone that's with them—there will be no place for them to hide." Several weeks after Moran was taken for his one way ride Frank Devlin, the football player turned bootlegger, was shot three times in the back of the head and then dumped on a farm near Summerville, New Jersey. Piteo was believed kidnapped off a Manhattan street, pumped full of lead, and then thrown into the Passaic River. His body was never found. Even Tom "fatty" Walsh, the former Rothstein bodyguard who reorganized his late boss's gambling syndicate, was shot to death after a card game at the Miami Biltmore Hotel. As the feud continued, Diamond settled old scores and saw to it that there would be no one left to implicate him in the murders. "We have to get every one of those rats and get complete control," Legs told his lieutenants, downing drink after drink. "There will be a big cut for you McDonald if you can get Moe and Harry first, they deserve everything that's coming to them." Joe McDonald, the powerfully built thug, picked up his

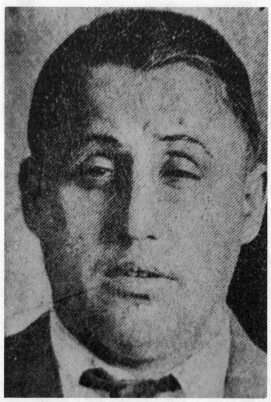

Moe Schubert, murdered by Diamond.

machine gun and holding it out in front of him interrupted Legs, "By the end of summer, I'll have most of them put away for good."

Diamond's gang started to clean up gangland with a vengeance. Small time thugs like Harry Vesey, Antonio Oliverio, Moe Schubert, Jimmy Ahern, and James Batto were shot in the head gangland style and their bodies dumped in New Jersey. All of them had long criminal records and a long time association with Diamond. Vesey, for example, was a short, spectacled gangster who had been arrested four times for murder. Given the same treatment he had shown to his victims, he was blackjacked, shot four times, and then thrown onto a main thoroughfare in Hoboken, New Jersey. Despite these successes, Legs

The car in which Eugene Moran's body was found.

Eugene Moran.

Diamond could not win his war. Waxey Gordon, Louis Buckhalter, "Gurrah" Shapiro, and Dutch Schultz made it too hot for him to continue his operations in the city and he fled to Acra.

In the summer of 1929, the major bootleggers and racketeers held a meeting at the Hotel President in Atlantic City, New Jersey to discuss the distribution of whiskey and the division of territory. Attending from New York were Meyer Lansky, Dutch Schultz, Owney Madden, Frank Costello, and Frankie Uale; from Philadelphia came Maxie Hoff; from Kansas City came Solly Weisman; from Chicago came Al Capone and Greasy Finger Guizak; from Detroit came Joe Bernstein and other members of the infamous Purple gang; and a host of others were present from several western cities. Legs Diamond, conspicuously absent, was on everyone's wanted list and preferred to stay in hiding.

With gangsters meeting in resort cities and gang killings increasing, the public wanted to know what could be done to stop the criminals. A *Colliers* editorial called for "aroused public sentiment" that would force the nation's mayors and police to fight crime. The *Saturday Evening Post* also put responsibility on the shoulders of the police, admonishing them to drive the criminals from the cities. With Diamond particularly in mind, the *Albany Evening News* said, "The State of New York should be able to end the blot of racketeering and gangdom within its borders . . . it can be ended and it must be." Legs Diamond was quick to reply to all this furor by saying that, he was "just a young fellow trying to get ahead, who wouldn't harm a flea."

3

Jack the Enterpriser

Women played a big role in Jack "Legs" Diamond's life and there was hardly a time when he did not have one or two around. Florence Williams, for example, a tall, slim brunette with heavily penciled eyebrows accentuating big brown eyes was quite an eyeful. As a waitress she was as popular as any girl that worked in the restaurants and chop houses that skirted the great white way. Although she was the favorite of sailors, stage-door Johnnies, and truck drivers, she liked the suave well-dressed "Legs" Diamond best. Dazzled by gifts of French perfume, furs, and fashionable clothes she became his steady girlfriend, and in the fall of 1917 became Mrs. Jack Diamond in a religious ceremony officiated by Father Otis Roche. But Florence Williams could not influence her husband to be loyal and loving. Legs was hardly at home, in their cheap apartment on the lower West Side, and when he did stay around he became thoroughly drunk. There were also other girls, the ones Eddie talked about and the ones she saw in the back seat of Legs' car. "I'll pray for you Jack. I'll pray for you. You no good tramp," she would shout at him. "Take me or leave me kiddo. I do what I want," Jack answered. Day in and day out they battled, with Florence threatening to report Jack's illegal activities to the police. "If you bring that blond hussey around

Alice Diamond.

here it will be the end of you, I mean it." Grabbing Flo by the arm, he replied mirthlessly, "Ha, Ha, you don't really mean that. If you do you will end up in the East River."

The marriage lasted only a few months and Florence Williams left Manhattan, a much disillusioned girl searching to find herself. Her recovery was quick and within a year she married a garage mechanic, settling for a much simpler life. In December 1931, immediately after the murder of "Legs" Diamond in an Albany rooming house, she surfaced again to comment to the press that, "Jack Diamond has passed completely out of my life. . . . I am sorry that he met his death the way he did, but he means nothing to me. I haven't made up my mind yet whether I will attend his funeral."

Long Island born Alice Kenny was one of the reasons Legs stayed out at night. A secretary and dance hall habitué she became Legs' second wife in 1926, being usually devoted but intolerant of his girlfriends. She is still remembered as a crass, nagging, beer guzzling ignoramus who could curse as well as a mule driver. Jack seldom argued with her, he remained calm or left the house to get a few drinks at a nearby roadhouse. Alice, about five feet four inches tall, plump, and five years younger than Jack, gambled, continued to drink heavily, and put on weight as her problems grew worse.

Alice's main problem was Marion Strasmick, the Ziegfeld Follies showgirl from Boston, popularly known as Kiki Roberts. In the twenties, every American knew that a Ziegfeld Follies girl was "desirable, beautiful, and breathtaking." The ingredients that went into such a gorgeous creature included natural hair color (if possible, big eyes of any color but gray, and the right face and figure. Born in 1909, Kiki Roberts was five feet four inches tall, weighed 118 pounds, had big beautiful brown eyes, a stunning figure, saffron hair, and a wiggle to her walk that stopped traffic. On the inside, though, she was described as "really low-down" or as "a foul-mouth, who was just no good." Every other word that came out of her mouth was obscene, and in this respect she and Jack were equal.

Marion Kiki Roberts was a bombshell on her way up in the tough, competitive world of showbusiness. She already had some minor success in the Follies in "Whoopee," "Simple Simon," and George White's "Scandals." In 1927 she was invited to stay on Broadway. She first met Jack at Texas Guinan's Del Fey Club in 1927 on the occasion of her celebrating the opening of a Broadway show.

If there was one thing Kiki liked best about Jack it was the way he spent money. One Friday afternoon in September, Jack took her to Franklin Simons where she spent more than five hundred dollars of his money on clothes. He stocked her apartment, in the East Sixties, with the most expensive furniture and knick knacks, and opened up charge accounts for her in several exclusive stores. Who else, but a Broadway gangster, could afford to cater to the whims and expensive tastes of Kiki. Their relationship was close and Jack even spoke of leaving Alice. In the cool autumn evenings they strolled in Central Park eventually ending up at the Roosevelt Grill at Madison Avenue and Forty-Fifth, where they danced to the music of the up and coming Guy Lombardo. Since dressing up was not essential and the crowd sedate, few people recognized Legs and Kiki and it was here they could be alone. Occasionally they would go up to Ben Riley's Arrowhead Inn on Riverdale Avenue and 246th Street, which boasted of a mixed clientele including many spenders from Broadway.

Alice was helpless when Kiki was around and continually pleaded with Jack to leave her. Interestingly enough, there were times when Alice and Kiki stayed in the same house in Acra, an unhealthy situation since both carried small pistols in their pocketbooks and exchanged threats to kill each other. The house staff always expected a gun battle, in which one or both would be killed and the whole place shot up. Alice, quite vehement about Kiki's presence, threatened, "I'll pull that little red-haired bastard apart if she doesn't get out of here. It will be just too bad for both of them." To be on the safe side, he arranged for the beautiful showgirl to be secretly housed at an Inn in Tannersville, several miles away from his Acra estate. Neither, of course, knew of a third girlfriend in nearby Saugerties, fourteen miles away, that Jack visited when he could. Rumors flew that he saw several more girlfriends when time permitted. Legs Diamond it appeared, was loyal to no one except his brother Eddie.

His Acra estate was convenient not only as a rest home for Eddie, but also for his extramarital affairs, and as a hideout from New York and Newark police. The small village of Acra, with only 300 souls, was situated high up in the Catskill mountains, some 155 miles from New York City. With several inns and hotels it took care of the tourist overflow from other parts of the county during the summer and fall. But when winter came it was as desolate as the barren wastes of the North Pole. Diamond especially liked Cairo and Durham which were popular vacation spots, for the Irish, for more than twenty years. To the west of Acra is Catskill, the county seat and the largest town in Greene County with its 5,000 population. To the east is the small village of Windham, now a popular winter resort, and to the northeast is Athens with its 2,500 population, once famous as a whaling port and for boat building. At the time, it was common to find that many of the area's residents were afflicted with tuberculosis and other respiratory ailments and had resided in the region in the hope that the cool mountain air would help them. Afflicted with tuberculosis was the Reverend Francis A. Kelley, once fighting Chaplain of the 27th division during the First World War, who was pastor of the Sacred Heart Church in Cairo and visiting pastor of the small church in Acra. He had lived in Cairo for more than eight years and was an important figure in the community and a source of inspiration to those similarly afflicted.

Father Kelley knew Legs well and visited his Acra home several times. Once, just after Legs' release from the Albany Hospital in May 1931, the good father drove out to Acra to pay his respects to the gangster. "My good friend Legs, haven't I told you that your ways are just no good. When are you going to change?" After offering Father Kelley a glass of Scotch, just smuggled in from Canada, which he refused, the gangster smiled and in a low pitched voice responded, "Father, the day I leave the rackets is near. I've got enough dough put away to do something else, like managing several prizefighters or something." "I sincerely hope so," said the cherubic priest. "How many more shootings can you stand? The Lord has been good to you for now. Maybe he has given you warnings. But will he be good to you next time? Watch out Legs." Legs Diamond, the casual Catholic, promised to go to church regularly and give up his life of crime.

Word of the cold mountain air must have reached Chicago, where matters were not going well for Al Capone. Capone and Diamond communicated frequently, with each other, on rum running matters and Diamond took a lively interest in Chicago's gang wars. In 1929, Legs went to Chicago to attend the funerals of the seven killed in the St. Valentine's massacre and to confer with Capone. During the late summer of 1930, real estate agents in Kingston reported contacts by the Capone organization to learn the best property in the Tannersville, New York area,

Legs Diamond's Acra estate in 1931. 1. His home; 2. bungalow used as a card and pool room; 3. small garage; 4. and 5. kennels housing vicious dogs; 6. ditch in back of home; 7. road to Catskill, New York; 8. road to Windham, New York; 9. pistol range; 10. house used by gang.

only a few miles from Diamond's estate. Newspaper reporters thought they were on to something real big when they learned that Diamond was also considering purchasing property in the same area.

Capone never came to Greene County, but others of his ilk did. The presence of gangsters increased tourism and several tourist maps depicted Diamond's estate on Route 23, marking it with the word "gangsters."

The center of tourist interest was Jack's seven room house, situated approximately 150 feet from the county road, but obscured by a dozen or more trees. Some one hundred feet west of the home was the care taker's cabin, and behind the house was a two car garage and a pool cottage. Inconspicuous from a distance, the place was actually a fortress. Atop the enclosed porch was a floodlight that covered the front of the house and situated in a nearby tree was another spotlight which shone directly on the open land west of the house. Two huge and thoroughly unfriendly police dogs roamed the grounds day and night, and if one looked closely he could see three or four burly men about the place. In 1930, an Albany newspaper reported that,

> several neatly screened and curtained windows look out of the front of the house. The caretaker's house is boarded up, the only sign of occupancy being a small hole in the wall directly beneath the peak of the roof in front, usually covered by a wooden shutter, but open during the threat of gang attacks two nights ago. A machine gun might easily spit a deadly fire across a wide range from this porthole.

Throughout the summer months, neighbors could hear the distinct rapid fire cracks of the Thompson sub-machine gun and knew that Jack's gang was taking target practice on milk bottles in a secluded area behind the house. When Jack was around there was always a small arsenal of weapons on the premises including several machine guns and a supply of hand grenades.

The interior of the house was considered elaborate, even by big City standards, with imported French wallpaper, solid mahogany furniture, and luxurious carpets trucked in from New York City's finest stores. A Negro maid lived on the premises

Left to right: Trooper Howard Rice, Cairo Police Chief Peter Christiansen, and Trooper Ed Updyke. Photo was taken just after raid on White's farm.

and several neighbors helped Alice with the household chores. In 1931 Legs had the whole place wallpapered and repainted, an event that many still remember. Harry Morrison, a Cairo paperhanger, recalls working almost two weeks putting the most expensive paper on the walls and the "extra special" treatment he received while he was at the house. Almost all the area's best plumbers and carpenters were employed there for almost a month, at wages that only a gangster could pay.

To his neighbors, Legs Diamond was viewed as a country gentleman known as Jack Hart, Jack Schiffer, or John Nolan. His real identity was not learned until the incident at the Hotsy Totsy Club in 1928. But by this time, he was already well entrenched in the county listing as his good friends Sheriff Milton Bailey, his successor Harold Every, and Floyd Jones, Acra's representative in the county legislature. Catskill, though, was a difficult town for him to control. Police Chief George

Klein, an ex-state trooper, who was usually depicted in the New York City newspapers holding a shotgun, could not be bought. Klein remembers well the day Legs approached him in Catskill saying, "A smart cop like you could get rich if he looked the other way at times. There is big dough in it for you. Where could you make such money?" Klein's teeth gnashed and he looked Legs straight in the eyes and replied, "You get the hell out of here. You can't buy me or any cop in the area. If you start any trouble here it will be the last trouble you make anywhere." Legs did not like the reply and was about to speak again when he saw the big, burly policeman put his hand on his .45 caliber sidearm. "Have it your way George, we will meet again," he countered and then left quickly, in his big Lincoln sedan. Chief Peter Christiansen, of the Cairo Police Department, was also approached but Legs got the same answer.

In the county, the State Police of Troop G out of Hudson made their presence known. Their patrols constantly monitored the traffic near Diamond's estate and kept a close watch on the illicit trade in applejack, whiskey, and beer. On one occasion Sergeant Francis Hillfrank singlehandedly arrested Diamond's cousin Jimmy Hart and chauffeur Jimmy Dalton on charges of drunken driving, personally throwing both of them into the county jail. Then there was the time when Sergeant Dewey Lawrence stopped Legs for speeding and found a concealed weapon in his car. Jimmy Wynne, proprietor of the Aratoga Inn in Cairo, New York said, "It was seldom that Jack did not leave his establishment dead drunk." On one cold January day in 1929, Legs lost control of his car ending up in a ditch. The impact of the accident set the car on fire and being dead drunk he was unable to extricate himself from the wreck. Fortunately for him, a passing farmer pulled him free and took him to the Catskill Police station. A doctor was called and because the incident occurred in the county, he was turned over to the State Police. Legs, still identifying himself as Jack Schiffer although his driver's license bore the name Diamond, paid a $50 fine for the drunk driving charge and a $15 fine for having an expired license.

Jack, Alice, or Kiki (depending upon his mood), and the bodyguards were frequently seen in the county. Bodyguard and

77

One of the planes used by Diamond.

chauffeur Jimmy Dalton drove Alice around in a huge tan Lincoln or blue Buick. Jack preferred to drive a tan Model A Ford or a green Oldsmobile. In late 1929 he took delivery on a custom built black Lincoln sedan that had several built-in compartments for sub-machine guns. The number and make of cars that Jack used changed frequently because they were involved in so many of his criminal activities.

Nearby at Leeds Airport was the "Legs Diamond air force," consisting of two airplanes belonging to Marvin Parks, a local barnstormer and charter pilot. Parks flew Diamond and his associates to Newark and Valley Stream Airports, the only two airports with lights, for $100, a good days pay at the time. Legs, always generous with money, usually threw in a $100 tip. The planes, with their powerful Wright-Waco engines and their tapered wing design, could carry between 600 and 700 pounds payload at speeds close to 80 miles per hour. According to Parks, Legs always looked forward to the plane ride and was constantly badgering him with questions about the plane's engine, speed, and power. He told the pilot, "Some day you'll teach me how to fly and then I'll buy a twin engine Lockheed." Countered Parks, "With the Lockheed, we could fly from Leeds all the way to Chicago without refueling." Parks could expect a call from Legs at almost anytime and he would have to drop everything for a trip to Chicago, Philadelphia, or New York City. Frequently, Diamond and his cohorts would fly to heavyweight championship prizefights or to close a big deal. The fact that Legs was in so many different cities, transacting business, indicates that he was no small time hoodlum. He had a hand in the major illicit activities in the country and had close contacts with every big time gangster, particularly Al Capone.

But no matter where he was, flamboyant, egotistical Legs was difficult to miss. He was the snappiest dressed gangster of the period and easily spotted in his custom-fitted dark suits, flashy ties, and black and white checkered cap. Driven around in a big limousine, accompanied by several tough bodyguards or walking arm in arm with red-haired Kiki Roberts, was enough to turn the heads of the impressionable upstate farmers. When he and Kiki attended the movies in Catskill, it became a subject of gossip everywhere. The two with as many as four bodyguards, occupied the central sector of the balcony at the small theatre displacing others who were already comfortably seated. Remembering Diamond's movie antics quite well one resident said, "He always seemed to be polite, even though he took over the whole place. He used to buy popcorn and candy for any kids sitting nearby and the kids really liked him." After the movies Jack took his entire entourage to any one of a number of road houses in the area, preferring either the Aratoga or Hollywood Inns. The Aratoga, managed by Jimmy Wynne, had a long bar in front and a large restaurant in the back. Upstairs there were about ten rooms that were rented to transients. A saxophonist, in the five piece Dixieland orchestra that played there nightly, remembered Diamond and Kiki quite well:

We listed him as a very fine man as sometimes he would slip us a couple of dollars to play a nice waltz for him and his girlfriend.

Many people visited the Inn just to see him and find out what he was like. They were usually impressed by his personality and fine appearance.

It was his generosity though, that made him popular with the area residents. In the summer of 1928 Legs sent his bodyguards rushing to Albany hospital with an injured woman who was six months pregnant and their quick action saved her life. It was Legs Diamond who put up most of the money for the construction of the small church in Acra and it was Legs Diamond who helped several impoverished farmers pay their bills. "God bless him, he saved my house and orchards," said one apple grower, who counted the gangster among his close friends. When he was in Catskill children flocked to his side for a handout, usually a few coins, but he never failed to respond.

The Robin Hood antics of Legs Diamond are remembered well by Phillip Thomas, who was the gangster's errand boy and part-time chauffeur in 1929. "If he liked to do anything at all it was to play Santa Claus to kids and old folks," said Thomas, who drove into Catskill on Legs' orders to pick up twenty dollars worth of candy for a little girl sick with scarlet fever. And he remembered the time that Legs established a hundred dollars credit at a Catskill department store for one Greene County woman who had lost all her clothes in a fire. Thomas drove Legs into town on Mondays in a big, tan Lincoln sedan. Sometimes, he would drive Legs to the Main Street barber shop where he would leave a five dollar tip. Most of the time, Legs was dressed only in an old pair of trousers, a lumberjack shirt, and a cap. Diamond liked caps and had about a dozen of them. It was the parties that Thomas remembers best, recalling that at one there were six or eight of his cronies up from New York City, some local politicians, a few pretty girls including Agnes O'Laughlin, Rudy Vallee's ex-girlfriend. Most of the time these tough guy gangsters, with their guns bulging out from underneath their jackets, sat around half drunk talking business, which to them was how many hauls of booze they took from one place to another. Thomas always spoke of Legs as being a gentlemen, and he tried to make everyone feel right at home. He was present at one of the parties when there was some unexpected excitement. The dogs gave the alarm by barking like hell and Jimmy Dalton came barging into the living room shouting that there was someone trying to get near the house. Thomas recalled clearly that,

> within a few seconds there were at least four armed men with Thompson sub-machine guns running out the back door toward the woods. A huge spotlight was turned on and directed toward the rear of the grounds. Rat-a-tat-tat, rat-a-tat-tat, the choppers probably could be heard in Catskill, but the bodyguards were just letting off some steam—no one could be found. All this time Legs sat calmly on the couch joking about how the boys would probably shoot each other before they shot anyone else. Saccio, fondling a hand grenade, was just waiting for the opportunity to blow someone to bits.

With a slight grin on his face Thomas recalled how Alice was always nagging Legs and the household help, frequently using vile language. He remembered the time he drove her, her sister, and a maid all the way to Kingston to see a Charlie Farrell film. On the way back they stopped off at Western's Chateau road house where the three took a table near the band while Thomas sat at the bar keeping them in sight. "After all, I had to get them back home safely or I could be shot. For this reason I turned down Harry Western's invitation to join a big card game upstairs, where some big shot gamblers from New York City who were taking on all comers."

What impressed Thomas and others close to Legs was the gangster's recklessness, flamboyance, and ruthlessness. He had contempt for the social order, for his competitors, and for those intimate with him. What caused his criminality? What forces molded him? The answers to such questions are not easily found. The belief that Diamond and those of his ilk were forced into crime by economic forces is not really valid. Although he came from a poverty stricken background and belonged to a suppressed but aggressive minority, so did many others and they did not lead lives of crime. In fact the Irish eventually achieved much material success, as did the Jews, the Norwegians and many other ethnic groups. Surely the lack of opportunity for these and other unassimilated groups was a factor in forcing many of them into crime, but it can never be proved to be the major factor.

The Marxist belief that criminal behavior resulted from a capitalist system that exploited the workers has little foundation. There is crime among all classes and groups in our society. And there is crime, lots of crime, in the socialist states of Europe.

Surely the belief, that he was a criminal because of certain physical attributes is also inapplicable. Today, no one seriously accepts Cesare Lombroso's theory that criminal tendencies were inherited or that the "born criminal" reveals certain physical characteristics that are really a throwback to a primitive type of man. Legs Diamond did not resemble Neanderthal man.

There is also the idea that physique is related to tempermental characteristics as an explanation for crime. One criminologist divided human beings into four basic physical types based on body measurements, but his criteria failed to take into consideration those who did not meet his tight standards and those that did, but did not respond as predicted.

Certainly Jack "Legs" Diamond could be called a socialized delinquent child—one who was influenced by bad companions, was a gang member, and who was a thief. His neglectful parents and truancy fom school are also symptoms underlying such a label.

But Legs Diamond was much more than a delinquent kid who came under bad influences. He had a true psychopathic personality that guided his actions, and although intelligent enough to succeed in legitimate undertakings, he elected to follow a career of crime. One indication of this was his inability to determine between truth and falsehood. Diamond lived in a world of lies, misrepresentations, and deceit. He cheated on his wives, his associates, and his relatives. He would constantly say, "I never did anything wrong," or "I'm just a young fellow trying to get ahead." The reasons behind the shooting at the Hotel Monticello certainly underlie this fact.

Prone to failures and setbacks, of which he had many, Jack failed to learn from his reverses. He repeated his mistakes and suffered the consequences. He was the only big time gangster to be shot down five times—the fifth time being fatal. He rarely took precautions and was known to go about on occasion without his bodyguards or without a gun. The night he was murdered he lacked both—even after he was warned that there were suspicious characters around.

Diamond, because he was a true psychopath, did not have the capacity for true love and was really incapable of forming lasting relationships. His first marriage was short-lived and his marriage to Alice was a sham. He even cheated behind Kiki's back and knew a number of girls intimately. He hurt all of them. His promiscuity was apparently a result of an unfulfilled sex life. He viewed Kiki and Alice not as partners with feelings but as objects. Legs Diamond lacked empathy and everyone knew his cruelty and insensitivity.

Surely by his words and deeds he tells us much about himself. He said he wasn't afraid of anything and once his mind was made up there was little that could be done to change it. "There is nobody anywhere, who is going to beat Legs Diamond," he would constantly boast. He was convinced that he should control a major share of the illegal booze and drug traffic in the eastern United States, no matter what the cost. But the truth of the matter was that as his share of the booze and drug market grew, the more he had to protect and worry about. He became more insecure and more defensive.

But, in spite of his psychological imperfections he proved himself to be an astute businessman. He became a banker and friend to many small time rumrunners, local politicians, and even the police. He was also able to practice public relations better than any other gangster of his day and it paid handsome dividends.

"For the right price you can buy any judge," he would say and proceeded to take advantage of a corrupt, deteriorating, and ineffective legal system. For the right price gangsters got away with robbery and murder, as Legs Diamond's record proves. Always taking advantage of a situation he knew that sympathy for his cause was national and in turn was viewed by many as a hero. The wets were a powerful force and needed him to get their supply of whiskey. At the same time he donated large sums of money to the prohibitionists, for without prohibition he would be put out of business. If anything he was a shrewd businessman and realizing that prohibition would not last, invested in prizefighting ventures and narcotics, two good bets for a gangster.

Although Jack spent much time in Greene County he was still actively involved in the New York City operations. What the yokels did not know, however, was that he was part of Arnold Rothstein's multi-million dollar drug peddling operation, the largest of its kind in the world. It was drug pushing that particularly interested Jack because of the huge profits, much more than could be made with bootleg booze. Joseph Murphy, a former narcotics agent who turned reporter for the *New York Daily Mirror* claimed that:

> If Jack Diamond had died his successor to the leadership of the mob would already be arranging to get these cargoes underway. Gang leaders may be killed, but the dope traffic goes on and always will go on, while the gold that is coined from the sufferings of poor addicts greases the palms of crooked officialdom.

Increased addiction among American servicemen after World War I created new fears, and in 1918 the New York State Commission of Narcotic Control was established with powers to regulate drug use in the state. But this action came too late, as drugs were readily available everywhere. It was not until Representative Stephen G. Porter of Pennsylvania successfully introduced HJR 195 in 1929 that measures were taken to ban the domestic manufacture of heroin by prohibiting the importation of crude opium. It was also through Porter's efforts that the Federal Bureau of Narcotics was established in 1930 and this streamlined the Bureau of Prohibition. Investigations were now more likely to be free from corruption and mismanagement, though the gangsters were practically untouched by these changes. They had close ties with the federal narcotics agents in New York City who were already known to be incompetent and derelict in their duty. Time and time again the big pushers got away, strongly indicating some sort of collusion between the agents and the gangsters.

The illicit market in drugs boomed during the twenties. Charles "Lucky" Luciano, an established dealer, was selling his drugs to Orientals and Europeans from the Mediterranean. By his own admission he was involved with every major dealer

State Troopers look over still they captured in a raid near Schenec-
tady, New York, 1929. Left to right: George Kerr, Sgt. Robert
Kelly, Charles Hill, Thomas Cornin, Lt. Harold Nagell.

in narcotics by 1923. On June 5 of that year he was arrested in
downtown Manhattan with six large packages of pure heroin
in his possession. Using his unique ability of making a deal
with the narcotics agents, he was able to get the charges
dropped. But he was harassed by the Bureau and forced to give
up narcotics for several years thereafter. Only the master criminal, Arnold Rothstein, was able to dominate the drug traffic
at this time. Rothstein, an opium smoker as a young man,
became so successful in narcotics peddling that "he was the
only man in the United States who could, and did, establish
a credit standing with foreign interests sending drugs into this

country." Throughout this period, he relied more and more on Diamond who reaped a fortune for himself as a contact and a seller. By the mid-twenties one kilogram (2.2 lbs.) could be purchased for $2,000 and sold for more than $300,000. Rothstein, at the time of his death, had between two and four million dollars tied up in his drug business that spanned across Europe and into South America.

In 1926 Rothstein sent Legs to Europe to make the necessary purchases and arrange for smuggling the narcotics into the United States. His efforts were successful and right under the

"When its Springtime in the Catskills."

noses of the customs agents heroin, morphine, and cocaine poured into the country inside small, stuffed animals delivered to Valentine's Importing Company on Walker Street in lower Manhattan. Ostensibly purveyors of oriental rugs, vases, and stuffed items it was an obvious front for Rothstein's huge drug operations. Drug peddlers came to the metropolitan area in droves to buy at Valentines, conducting their business right under the noses of the police who, in many instances, were themselves involved in dope peddling. A raid, by a special intelligence unit in July 1928, on police department lockers resulted in some seven detectives being caught with the goods. Eventually almost fifty detectives became involved in one of the biggest shakeups in police department history.

The trafficking in dope aroused the suspicions of many. Approximately fourteen months after Rothstein's death United States Attorney Charles Tuttle and his assistant John Blake were able to tie to Rothstein and Diamond such important officials as Colonel L.G. Nutt, Chief of the Federal Narcotic Bureau in Washington, D.C., his son Rolland, his prominent lawyer, son-in-law L.P. Menningly, and George W. Cunningham, the federal narcotics agent in charge of the metropolitan New York district. In a statement to the press Blake said, "Startling evidence involving figures in New York public and private life, and disclosing more fully Arnold Rothstein's overlordship of the narcotic rings in the United States, will be presented to the federal grand jury . . ." However, pressure from powerful politicians quickly put an end to the proposed revelations and nothing further was ever heard of the matter again. At the same time a half dozen New York City police officers, of high and low rank, were accused of concealing evidence in the investigation into the Rothstein murder. Obviously those involved with Rothstein had stopped at nothing to protect themselves.

Among the more important figures to get involved with Diamond and Rothstein was Captain Alfred Loewenstein, the millionaire, Belgian financier. In 1928 he came to New York City to negotiate with both men what was probably the biggest drug transaction in the country up to that time. In a suite of rooms in an East 42nd Street hotel, the three surrounded by aides and bodyguards argued for hours over prices and dis-

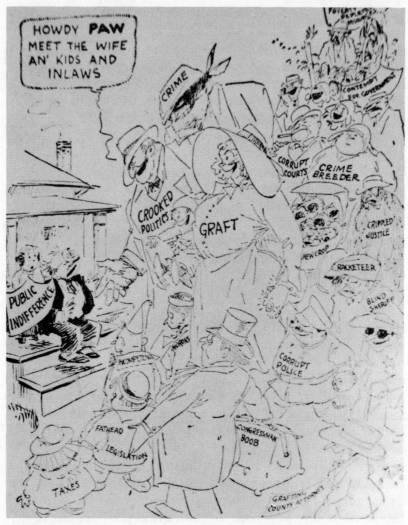

"A homecoming may be a good thing now and then to get acquainted with our offspring."

Behind the criminal, the crooked lawyer.

tribution rights. At one point the bargaining got so heated that
Loewenstein had to be quieted by his aides. "God damn it,"
shouted Legs, "what the hell do you want. Everyone gets an
even share or there will be lots of lead flying around here."
Loewenstein pushed his two bodyguards aside and staring right
into Diamond's eyes said, "You can't get the narcotics without
me and I'll get the cut I ask for." Everyone was silent for a
full three minutes. Then Rothstein spoke, "Gentlemen, gentlemen, let us be calm, surely there is enough profit in the business
for everyone." Somehow or other a deal was made and the
mysterious Loewenstein left New York City quite content with
having a big say in the international narcotics market. The fact
that Loewenstein, the third richest man in the world, was
involved with the likes of Rothstein and Diamond indicated
the magnitude of drug operations at this time. Loewenstein, a
Jew who had converted to Catholicism, never disclosed the
source of his wealth. At the time he maintained his own air
force of twenty-four planes and was rich enough to offer the
Belgian government a loan of $40,000,000 without interest. He
died under the most unusual circumstances in July 1928, falling
4,000 feet from his own airplane while it was crossing the
North Sea from England to Belgium. British police, after a
prolonged investigation, were never able to give a satisfactory
answer for his death which still remains a mystery.

Legs' future hinged on the control of drug operations after Rothstein's death. His failure to raise enough money to carry on the importation and sale of drugs, his constant drinking, his lack of organizational ability, and his ongoing feuds with other gangsters blocked his chances for success. Time and time again he would continually tell Alice, "I think I can pull it off. I think I can get control of the whole drug empire in America, if not next year then soon." He had to have the contacts and turned to Robert Miller, alias "the Count," and Abraham Laimas, new associates with an organization reaching right into Europe. Miller was useful for his contacts with Teutonic Chemists, a German manufacturer of synthetic drugs that was supplying the American market for the right price. Legs, now flat broke, could not raise the money to close a deal with them. As a result he sought to make a speedy withdrawal from the Clinton Avenue

Legs Diamond being brought in for questioning in the Newark bank robbery by the New York City Police.

branch of Newark's South Side Bank and Trust Company. On June 7, 1930, he and four others made off with $14,000 in cash, a surprisingly small sum and certainly not enough with which to do business. Bank employees quickly told authorities that they saw a red-headed woman in the back seat of the getaway car and later picked out Diamond's picture from the rogue's galley photographs. Legs, Miller, and Laimas were immediately picked up at the Hotel President, of West 48th Street, and booked for armed robbery. It was Diamond's twenty-third arrest and he took the whole matter very lightly. Legs surely knew how to deal with witnesses, especially after the Hotsy Totsy experience.

Questioned by detectives he denied knowledge of any murders in Newark or of the bank robbery, declaring that he was an "automobile salesman who was temporarily unemployed." This response brought a roar of laughter from the police. The three prisoners were then put into a lineup where seven witnesses to the robbery tried to identify them. Face to face with one of the most notorious criminals in the country and a known murderer, they quickly changed their minds about their previous identification. William Lyman, counsel for the three men, then asked for an immediate hearing and within twenty-four hours the trio was released. Diamond's preparations for his European trip continued, but now he had new help.

Salvatore Spitale, Legs' close ally in crime and a long time member of the gang, sought to raise the much needed money. Born in Italy in 1897, he came to this country with his mother and brother Peter when he was six years old. Eventually he ended up in the village of Leeds in Greene County, where his mother operated a small hotel. As previously stated, it was Salvatore who persuaded Legs to come to Greene County and it was Salvatore who guided much of the criminal activity that Legs was associated with. Tall, slim, and roundfaced with a tan complexion, the snappily dressed gangster had a part interest in several speakeasies, in the Hotel Richmond on west 46th Street and in a hotel in Newark, New Jersey. For most of his life he managed to stay clear of the law being arrested in 1931 for carrying an unlicensed revolver, for which he later produced

Salvatore Spitale.

a permit. But, in 1939 he stole $10,000 from a business partner and spent it at a race track. For this he received five years in Sing Sing.

Spitale's contacts went deep into the underworld and he was able to persuade a hoodlum named Irving Bitz, a vicious racketeer who owned several speakeasies, to raise $200,000 for Legs. More than half of this money came from underworld speculators, including a sizeable sum from Al Capone. In physical appearance the professorial looking Bitz was short, thin, round-faced, and wore thick glasses. He had been arrested ten times since 1922 and was convicted once, in 1927, of violating the Harrison Drug Act for which he was sentenced to Sing Sing for a period of three to six years. But, he was released on good behavior in twenty-seven months and quickly returned to his life of crime.

Bitz and Spitale were no ordinary crooks. Their ties to major underworld figures were well known, and this was a factor behind Charles and Anne Lindbergh appointing them as go betweens in the famous Lindbergh kidnapping case. A notice that appeared in the newspapers on March 5, 1933, placed by the Lindberghs read:

92

If the kidnappers of our child are unwilling to deal direct, we fully authorize "Salvy" Spitale and Irving Bitz to act as our go betweens. We will also follow any other method suggested by the kidnappers that we can be sure will bring the return of our child.

Unfortunately for all concerned, these two did not know who kidnapped the Lindbergh baby and the police turned their efforts toward finding an amateur instead of a professional criminal. More will be said of Spitale and Bitz later on.

4

Where is Harry Western?

The gangster's stock rose as millions of thirsty Americans continued to sip whiskey, guzzle beer, and openly carry flasks in their hip pockets. Even Vice-President Charles Curtis was accused by the former prohibition administrator of New York of having used his influence in "causing alcohol permits to be issued." With the widespread breakdown of enforcement and police morality the booze flowed into the city by truck convoys. The dries pressed their case, and a few honest policemen and prohibition agents made some raids while the gangsters struggled among themselves for prime territory.

With Rothstein dead, the competition for the whiskey and drug empire became fierce with few interludes of peace. The aggressive Dutch Schultz muscled in on Owney Madden, Diamond, Vincent Coll, and even Augie Pisano, who was Al Capone's New York City representative. During the summer of 1930, New York City became an armed camp as gangsters carrying machine guns, shotguns, and rifles protected beer trucks and speakeasies.

Diamond, determined to strike back, had gathered a small army to smash the competition. He was supported in this venture by the boisterous and flashy Vannie Higgins, his pal in so

Huge arsenal belonging to Jack "Legs" Diamond seized by New York City Police in August 1930.

many illegal operations. "Lets do it right, Legs. Lets get every one of them," blurted Higgins. Turning toward his pal and handing him a box of hand grenades, Legs responded, "We have to get Schultz and his gang first. Bombs and grenades are the only thing that will work. We have to blow all of them up at the same time." Vannie and Legs, laughing aloud, then went about setting out stakeouts on Schultz's hangouts. But something went wrong. In August, police sources got a tip that Diamond had assembled a huge arsenal in a Brooklyn apartment, and in the raid that followed found the "largest cache of arms, ammunition, and defensive equipment ever discovered in the city." Among the confiscated arms were eighteen hand grenades, five home-made bombs, three tear gas bombs, one gallon of tear gas, twenty-two fountain pen pistols, four Very signal pistols, four Maxim silencers for pistols, sixteen machine gun clips, six Thompson sub-machine guns, and a handbook on

A rum runner's fortress mansion, formerly the property of Oscar Hammerstein, near Highlands, New Jeresy.

how to use the Thompson. Taken into custody in the raid were James Dalton, Diamond's trusted chauffeur, and his always loyal aide Harry "Skunky" Klein.

Without his guns and bombs Diamond was helpless in the city, and had to call off his planned St. Valentines Day type massacre prepared for Schultz and his gang. His brief alliance with Pisano, Coll, and Higgins added substance to the stories of massive killing and demonstrated the serious state of affairs in New York's gang world. In the meantime he strengthened his hold upstate, making Greene County his base of operations. His gang of beer runners and musclemen terrorized local bootleggers and roadhouse proprietors, beat up truck drivers, and stole whole cargoes of beer and whiskey. Entire stills were demolished with machine guns and establishments not purchasing Diamond's very inferior beer were wrecked. In one instance the Elks Club in Catskill was visited by Diamond's gangsters, who shot up the bar and several beer kegs. The method was always quite simple. An innkeeper from Leeds remembers well the time Garry Saccio and three tough guys came into his place armed with axe handles. "Look here Coaley," said Saccio. "We heard you have been buying Madden's beer. We don't want to hear such things. You'll take beer from us at our prices or we'll break your God-damned head." The defenseless innkeeper, unaccustomed to big time gangsters, complied. "I don't want any trouble boys, I am sure we can do business." Coaley promised them anything, for he knew that Saccio was capable of breaking up a place and putting its owner in the hospital. Diamond's activities extended all the way to the Canadian border, where he arranged for the smuggling of high grade whiskey across the border in trucks that then carried their prized cargoes to New York City. His cheap beer, made in several breweries and by dozens of cooperating bootleggers, could be found in ten upstate counties.

A key link in this organization was Harry Western, owner of the Chateau, a popular road house in Lake Katrine, just a few miles from Kingston, the county seat of Ulster County. Originally from Jersey City, New Jersey and from a respected family that included fireman and policeman brothers, Western was able to

Agents examine weapons seized at mansion in Highlands, New Jersey.

Agent listens in on radio set found in mansion.

Harry Western's Chateau road house, Lake Katrine, New York, 1927.

maintain the image of a law abiding citizen and at first very few had knowledge of his criminal activities. Of average height, brown haired, and brown eyed, he was lithe, springy, and muscular with a penchant for horses and gambling. He was a key figure in the distribution of whiskey and beer in the upstate New York area since 1927, coming into contact with the most notorious bootleggers in the region. His Chateau restaurant, situated on the Kingston-Saugerties road, was considered the liveliest place in the Hudson valley, attracting patrons from great distances. Within, the lights were low and there was a long, veneered mahogany bar with a brass foot rail, and several highly polished spitoons. The walls were painted a light green and were hung with four huge paintings of pastoral scenes. In stark contrast to this, hanging directly over the bar was the multi-colored lithograph of Custer's Last Fight. The restaurant, occupying the larger half of the building was dimly lit and subdued in color. The walls were trimmed with mahogany veneered woodwork. Six large multi-bladed fans hung from the ceiling, twirling only inches from the patrons, while nearby there was a large hardwood dance floor that could hold fifty couples. Adjacent to it was a platform which held a six piece Dixieland band that played tunes like "That's My Weakness

Underground storage tank found at mansion.

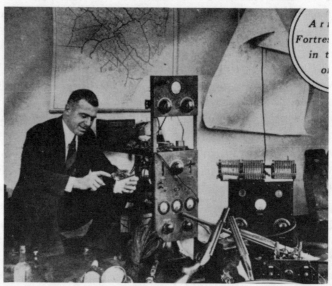

Agent looks over radio sending set and guns found in mansion.

Now" and "I'm the Sheik of Araby." Downstairs in the basement there were always sixty to eighty kegs of beer and twenty to thirty cases of whiskey ready to be shipped to eager buyers.

As an associate of Diamond, he became important to the Prohibition Bureau and it is believed by many, that to protect himself, he passed tips to bureau agents that resulted in the seizure of several important stills. Area bootleggers suspected Western and when still after still was closed down, Diamond ordered the killing of Western's pal Big Mike, a beer runner from Signac, New Jersey, who was in deep trouble with the Prohibition Bureau.

Western was next on the list. "That two-timing bastard has got to go, he is fouling up our operations all over," Diamond could be heard shouting over and over. On Saturday evening August 22, 1930 he was called to Diamond's estate at Acra and then, attended a huge bootlegger's party held at a hotel in Haines Falls, a short distance away. Reporters heard that it was the biggest and wildest party ever thrown in the history of the

State Troopers search a Model T Ford for illicit alcohol, on the Schoharie-Greene County border, 1921.

area. Wine and whiskey flowed like water and there were girls for everyone. Right after the celebration Western was lured to his car and shot to death. Reports that he was missing were circulated among area law enforcement officers. Within a few days they combined forces to launch the biggest search ever conducted for a missing person in the northeast. Throughout Greene and Ulster counties deputy sheriffs, state troopers, village and town police, and a multitude of volunteers combed the area for clues. Almost every pond and lake in the region was dragged including several lakes and streams that fed the Ashokan Reservoir. But no traces of the bootlegger could be found. Western's two brothers joined with Mrs. Western to offer a $5,000 reward for information leading to his whereabouts.

During this time, police agencies upstate and in New York

City kept a close watch on Diamond's haunts and their watch-fulness paid off. New York City detective Francis McCarty led a raid on a Brooklyn garage, located on 61st street next to a garage owned by Diamond's associate, Vannie Higgins, and across the street from the apartment in which the much pub-licized arsenal was seized. Found inside the garage was Harry "Skunky" Klein standing along side Harry Western's Buick. Upstate police now suspected there would be evidence at Dia-mond's estate. Within hours of Klein's arrest, some thirty state troopers assisted by Greene County deputy sheriffs and New York City Police Department detectives surrounded the gang-ster's home. With guns drawn, they approached the front door, and were met by Mrs. Diamond and two maids. Alice, when presented with a search warrant, responded, "You no good fuckin bastards, you can never leave us alone, you get the hell

State Troopers on patrol near Albany, 1925.

out of here." While still shouting obscenities, she was pushed aside and the police poured into her house. Within minutes of this confrontation state police photographers took the magnificent photograph on page 104, depicting Sheriff Harold Every, Sergeant Dewey Lawrence and several state troopers standing in front of Diamond's home. A quick search of the house and grounds revealed nothing but a hidden stairway. During the search the New York City detectives threw acid on the rugs and wallpaper and made some derogatory remarks to Mrs. Diamond, behavior undoubtedly brought on by old grudges against Jack, which was a surprise to the troopers and deputies.

At the Brooklyn garage a police investigation found blood-stains on the Buick's front seat, indicating that someone, probably Western, was shot either from the side or behind. Blood-stains about the car indicated that the luckless innkeeper was dragged from the front seat and disposed of somewhere else. The remains of Harry Western have never been found, but there is good reason to believe that he was buried on a lonely stretch of road, about to be paved, just outside of Catskill, New York.

Klein and Dalton were already in trouble with the law over the confiscated arsenal, but were later released by Brooklyn Judge Mark Rudich to a contingent of state troopers and deputy sheriffs who took them to Kingston. The handcuffed prisoners were placed in one car while two other cars loaded with machine gun toting lawmen, one following and one leading, escorted them on their way.

During his arraignment, Klein was charged with grand larceny in the theft of Western's car and Dalton was held as a material witness. "They'll never get anything on me," boasted the insipid Klein. He shouted at his jailers, "Legs will get me out of this, I know he will." A twenty-four hour guard was maintained around the county jail, as rumors flew that Diamond would break his men out. Everyone was on edge and there hadn't been such excitement in Kingston since the British burned the place down in 1777.

At the trial, Detective McCarty told the court that Klein admitted to him that he was asleep on the front porch of Diamond's house in Acra, where he was awakened by a man

Sheriff Harold Every, Undersheriff Milton Bailey, Sgt. Dewey Lawrence, and other Troopers on porch of Diamond's Acra home just after big raid. Note floodlight under peak of roof.

named McNamara who asked him to drive the car to the Brooklyn garage where a Fred Witcher would meet him and tell him how to dispose of it. He was given fifty dollars, twenty-five of which was to go to Witcher. Klein was preparing to dump the car into the river, when he was caught. The jury believed the police, and Klein was convicted of grand larceny.

As investigators put together the bits and pieces of Western's disappearance, it was learned that other inn keepers were also in trouble. The *Kingston Daily Freeman* reported that Harry Western was one of a number who had been marked by gangsters as victims:

Others in the locality have been spotted and apparently are on the list to be taken for a ride. Several places have been visited by gangsters and notified either to get in line for the proper source for their beer or beware. Many places have closed up and the proprietors of other places are in doubt as to the consequences.

Despite a vigilant state police, Diamond's gang roamed at large and the missing Harry Western became a symbol of gangster brutality.

"I'm not going to be pushed around by anyone, Saccio, Quattrochi, or whomever they send against me," boasted Joseph Hoy, of Catskill. Hoy, the proprietor of a fleet of trucks used

Left to right: Sgt. Francis Hillfrank, Sheriff Harold Every, and Sgt. Dewey Lawrence.

by a grocery chain, was approached by Garry Saccio who demanded $1,500 in cash, and if he did not pay within five days, he would have his garage and trucks blown up. Undaunted the truckman reported the extortion attempt to the police and told his friends, "They'll never get a cent from me. I'll take two of them with me before I go." Saccio, the archetypical bodyguard —tough, strong and good with a gun—could be counted on to carry through on his threats. "Saccio is a little lamb without his guns," said Chief Klein, "but with them he is a one man army." Saccio was indicted and Hoy knew he was in real danger. One afternoon he decided to take matters into his own hands and rammed his truck into Diamond's huge bulletproof limousine on Catskill's Main Street. Diamond, Saccio, and Dalton managed to escape injury, but the car was demolished. Only the presence of a midday crowd and the speedy arrival of the police saved Hoy from being shot down right then and there.

Jack "Legs" Diamond decided to get far away from all of this trouble. He boarded an ocean liner headed for Europe, carrying out his plan to bring large quantities of narcotics into the United States from Germany. For almost three weeks his activities on and off the ship were front page copy for every major newspaper in this country and England. And all this time the New York City authorities and the state police were seeking him for questioning in the Western case. British newspapers were particularly excited about Diamond and carried stories of "big, bad Jackie" coming to Europe. Scotland Yard alerted the Irish Minister of Justice that Diamond was aboard the *Baltic*, and they were directed to detain him for questioning in a stock swindle. According to rumor, it seems that Diamond advanced $50,000 to the notorious Jake "the barber" Factor to travel to Europe. Barber, in turn, cheated Englishmen out of $6,000,000. The mystery deepened when the captain of the *Baltic* wired back that Diamond was not on his ship.

A thorough check of all passenger liners at sea turned Jack up on the *Belgenland*, on which he and his two friends booked passage just before it sailed from New York. When the word got out, a large crowd of spectators gathered at Plymouth awaiting to see the gangster from America who had killed so many of his rivals. As the ship docked, a contingent of British

Sgt. Dewey Lawrence, holding notebook, confers with Undersheriff Milton Bailey and Sheriff Harold Every, during search for Harry Western, August 1930.

police boarded it and advised Jack that he would not be permitted to set foot on English soil. Newspaper reporters rushed aboard and found their subject responsive to their questions, "Now look, all I want is to go to Vichy for the cures and to stage a fadeout. I have stomach and liver troubles and I have been told to come here and take the waters." Upon questioning the passengers, reporters learned that he was using the alias John T. Nolan and was quite a successful gambler who made several thousand dollars playing poker. During his idle hours he was observed autographing menu cards and shaking hands with elderly ladies.

The Belgian authorities were similarly hostile and when

Law officers searching for Harry Western, August 1930.

the ship docked in Antwerp, Jack was detained twenty-four hours pending word on what to do with him from the Minister of Justice. Meanwhile, several squads of riot police lined the streets around the pier awaiting developments. Thoroughly annoyed and wearing a bedraggled look, Jack was ushered through customs, past reporters and a large crowd of curious onlookers to city hall, where the issue of his stay in Belgium was decided. The authorities, desiring to wash their hands of the whole matter, gave the illustrious American gangster a choice of three countries to go to and Legs, without hesitation, selected Germany. Belgian police put him on the Ostend-Vienna Express sitting with him until the train arrived at Aix-la-Chapelle, a frontier town. Here, German police took him into custody under the pretext of holding him for American authorities. At this time they received word that New York City Police were no longer interested in him and this complicated matters. To prevent an embarrassing situation from arising it was decided to deport Legs, but they could not find a steamship that would take him to the United States.

Several days of searching finally produced rooms on the German freighter *Hanover* at berth in Hamburg. "This is one hell of a way to treat an American," said Legs, who promised to do something about German hospitality. Retaining the prominent Hamburg lawyer Dr. Wilhelm Sandak, he commenced legal proceedings against the Prussian government. Demanding that he be repaid expenses for his trip from the United States and that he be given "smart money" for the wounds he received to his feelings by his detention in a Prussian jail. He also demanded to be indemnified for the harm done to his credit. Dr. Sandak claimed that he had a good case, because the United States and the Prussian police expressly disclaimed having any interest in Diamond's detention and there had been no demand for his extradition. Sandak noted that Diamond had a visa from the German consulate in New York. If the German authorities considered Diamond an undesirable foreigner, contended the lawyer, they should have refused him a visa. As the *Hanover* sailed into the Atlantic, its telegraph sent and received messages between Legs and his lawyer. Diamond still

Looking for Harry Western near Cairo, New York.

hoped that he could hop an eastbound freighter should his legal efforts prove successful.

The events in Europe had turned Legs Diamond into an internationally known figure. *The New York Daily News* paid particular attention to his activities and in an editorial entitled "Diamond—A Threat to Europe" which featured a picture of the gangster, declared,

Diamond said that he planned to go to Belgium where he would work out an idea "with my boys." He said that he did not plan to hurt anyone in Europe. . . . Europe need not worry much about the probability of Diamond's hurting anyone over there unless by chance he decides to survey the prospects in Finland . . . Finland's bootleggers are said to have their racket under excellent control and well guarded against chislers from the outside. . . . Diamond and men like him will probably go on being the growths peculiar to the United States.

110

Exhausted Troopers in the woods near Cairo, New York.

Finland, said the *News*, was the only nation in Europe which was dry, and that European countries handle the liquor problem by sane and profitable methods of government sale, by high liquor taxation, and strictly enforced closing hours.

Diamond, the subject of many editorials, had become moralistic in defense of his own criminality and the public came to adore him. In an editorial entitled "A Hoodlum Hero", *The Philadelphia Public Ledger* attacked the gangster:

> Time was when the very fact he was a city hoodlum would have convicted Diamond in the Catskills. Now he and his kind seem to have become the favored symbols of defiance of an unpopular law. And the very countrymen who once were the backbone of conservative law observance cheered him and set him free. Obviously the breakdown of the law includes more than corrupt police and complacent judges.

State Troopers and prohibition agents look over captured still near Diamond's estate at Acra, October 1929.

The legend of Diamond had grown to the point where many saw him as the lead figure in an American Arthurian legend. He was to be met on his arrival at Philadelphia by several civic-minded organizations, among them a group of Philadelphia society women. "We want to meet the man who's changing history. Legs Diamond is really a friend of individual liberty, for every man has a right to drink what he pleases," uttered a spokeswoman for one group. Preparations to greet the gangster were reaching a climax and produced a furor in the Quaker City, with the newspapers again carrying editorials and many letters to the editor. In response, the local chapter of the Women's Christian Temperance Union promised to picket the gangster at the pier and distribute leaflets condemning drink.

On September 22, the S.S. *Hanover* sailed into Philadelphia and Diamond was welcomed instead by a large delegation of Philadelphia police, who promptly escorted him to city hall

State Trooper on patrol in 1925. Vehicle carries truck-weighing scales.

to be questioned. "I haven't done anything wrong," said Legs, "this is just a lot of newspaper publicity. I was born and raised right here in Philadelphia. Why can't you treat me right?" Following a hearing, the next day it was decided to put Legs on a train for New York City and be rid of him.

Newspaper reporters and newsreel cameramen had a field day with this modern day black knight. It became a spectacle whenever a gangster like Diamond showed his face in public. Pedestrians strained their necks to see him and traffic stopped right in its tracks. The influence of gangsters on the young was particularly great and a popularity poll, taken in the late twenties, included Al Capone high on he list. It has been reported that thousands of spectators at the Charleston, Indiana Racetrack cheered Al Capone when he appeared with his bodyguards, waving his clasped hands above his head like a prizefighter entering a ring. At a Chicago Cub baseball game he was photographed with State Senator and later U.S. Con-

113

gressman Roland Lebonatti. And a short time later with Mayor
Bill Thompson of Chicago and the Italian aviator Italo Balbo.
During a football game between the University of Nebraska
and Northwestern University, in Evanston, Illinois, a group of
boy scouts shouted, "Yea Al." For the same reasons, Diamond
also attracted groups of youths and in one instance received
a bottle of healing lotion from an eight year old, Reading,
Pennsylvania girl, who hoped to help her hero.

If Capone was the darling of the masses in the midwest,
Diamond was his counterpart in the northeast. The *Literary
Digest* stated, "In France, Diamond's visit substituted him for
"Scar-Face Capone" as a symbol of the mad bootlegging scene,
where cafe settlers endow him with romantic qualities." In
England, the prestiguous *Manchester Guardian* likened him to
a rival Chinese bandit chief:

State Troopers ready to go into action, spring 1920.

114

When one set of criminals can announce publicly their intention of killing another and carry out that intention in the full glare of newspaper publicity, the general prestige of those responsible for law and order must inevitably suffer . . . The fate of Jack Diamond is without significance in itself. The social attitude toward him is significant of much.

Period newsreels reflected popular attitudes toward Diamond. By 1930, Movietone News had direct sound and was able to bring Legs Diamond's voice to thousands of Americans everywhere. In one sequence, taken as he is escorted out of Philadelphia in September 1930, Legs is asked by an inquiring reporter, "Was your trip a success Legs? Did you get what you were after?" Legs turned, and with a snarl replied, "You fellows know I went to Europe for my health. You aren't trying

Vannie Higgins.

to pin something on me are you? You can tell the public that most of what they have been reading about me is all bunk. I've got alot of legitimate interests." In another newsreel two policemen stand on the running boards on each side of a police car while four other officers are seated inside the vehicle with Diamond, which moved slowly through a large crowd of onlookers. One cameraman was able to film Diamond while he was escorted by police and reporters to a waiting train in the Philadelphia station. In both films he is well dressed and talkative. His left arm hangs limply at his side, this the result of one of the attempts on his life. Always there was much adulation. One observer said that the fascination which badmen like Diamond exert upon us may be an emotional safety valve. "We sin vicariously when we read of their exploits in the newspapers. When they have been tried and condemned, both our civilized sense of justice and our barbaric protest against the restraint of government are satisfied."

Within six weeks of his return from Europe, Diamond was again in the headlines. At 10:00 a.m. Sunday, October 12, at New York's Hotel Monticello he was shot down for the third time and became the sixty-ninth gangster to be shot down in New York City that year. The facts behind this shooting, though, were not revealed until about a year and a half later in a little known book entitled *Gimme*. The author, Emmanuel H. Lavine, a well-informed and aggressive reporter for *The New York Daily Mirror*, claimed that Legs was the victim of his old friend Vannie Higgins, whom he had double-crossed. Diamond, so Lavine says, took $50,000 to locate and safely return a gangster named Leo Steinberg. Leo and his brother, Jacob, were well-to-do businessmen and bootleggers protected by Augie Pisano's gang. Vannie Higgins responded by taking Leo for a one way ride, pumping his body full of bullets and then tying weights to it, and throwing it into the ocean near Long Beach, Long Island. Jacob, in a desperate state and unaware of his brothers fate, offered Legs Diamond $50,000 cash if he would use his influence among the underworld on Leo's behalf. "Give me the $50,000 Jake and I'll take care of things," said Diamond, who then contacted Higgins for assistance. Higgins finally told Legs the real whereabouts of Leo demanding, "I'll take the $50,000

Legs Diamond being escorted out of the 125th Street police station, November 1930.

all for myself. Jack, you do what you can to get the money from Jacob and don't give me any trouble or it will be too bad for you." Legs, of course, grabbed the $50,000 for himself and that is where matters stood until October 12, when the Higgins gang confronted him.

"You have one hour to raise the $50,000, Legs, or we start shooting," shouted Higgins' tough lieutenant. Three hours passed and Legs could only produce $25,000. Infuriated, Higgins' gunman pumped two bullets into Legs' side as a warning, making it clear that he would return for the remaining amount.

Legs received temporary medical treatment and spent several hours trying to recover his strength. Higgins' gang returned and after seeing that Legs did not have the money, pumped three more bullets into the gangster's now much riddled body. Diamond staggered out of his room and collapsed in the elevator. Hotel guests and employees carried him to a suite of rooms occupied by hotel manager Jacob Ginsberg. "Nobody can kill Legs Diamond, nobody can kill Legs Diamond," the tough gangster screamed at the guests. An ambulance was called and Dr. Howard Babcock, Diamond's New York City physician, rushed to the scene. Both arrived simultaneously, and after a quick look rushed the apparently dying gangster to Polyclinic Hospital. Although pale and bleeding profusely, Diamond asked for a few shots of whiskey, in addition to the three he already had, to bolster his strength for the ride in the ambulance.

Listed in serious condition the surgeons went right to work on him. There were bullet wounds in his right thigh, in the left side of his abdomen, two through the chest near the right and left armpits, and one in the center of his forehead. The last bullet apparently hit Legs as he reeled backwards and it

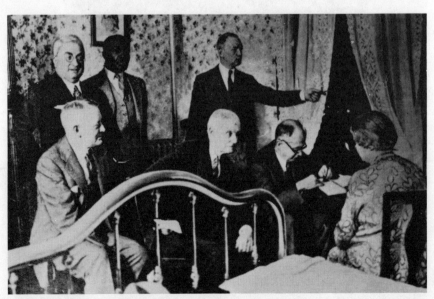

District Attorney and police officials look over the hotel room in which Diamond was shot, October 15, 1930.

just lacerated his scalp without touching his skull. One hospital physician stated, "Mr. Diamond has stomach ulcers and weak lungs and is in a very bad way." The question of whether Diamond had tuberculosis is debatable as symptoms did not appear either before or after this shooting. If he had anything at all, it was a powerful resistance to infection and a strong will to live. In the days before antibiotics, wounds were cleaned and dressed frequently and the patient's resistance played an important part in his recovery. Diamond was lucky again. The .38 caliber bullets were removed from his body and within a week his condition improved—quite a feat for a man of Diamond's lean physique.

The police, fearing another attempt on his life, ordered that he be removed to Welfare Island where they could set up better protective measures. Just as he was getting settled in his new quarters he was visited by the famous socialite Cornelia Biddle, of the Philadelphia Biddles, who just wanted to see what he was like. "Really, he is such a nice little fellow, he's so sweet, and such an intelligent sort of person, isn't he," said Cornelia. The *Daily News* said, "The leader in the best of New York's sets called on the leader of the worst of New York's sets." For Jack Diamond it was just another day and some more publicity.

During this time the newspapers had a field day. The *Buffalo Courier Express* claimed that, "The mention of a Follies

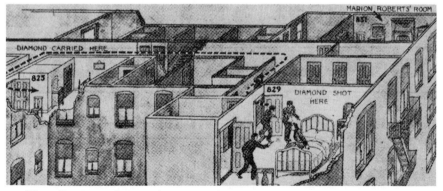

The diagram shows the room layout on the eighth floor of the Hotel Monticello, where Diamond was shot.

beauty, Broadway night life, and the sinister overpowering shadow of chance is the living law of every racketeer's existence. These features combined to make that tale of destruction of New York's best known racketeer everybody's business." *The New York World* echoed similar sentiments claiming that for ten years Diamond has been in one hot spot after another. "Between rival gangsters and the police, Legs has undoubtedly the honor of being the most harassed individual in New York's underworld." "The shooting of Diamond," says the editor of the Hartford *Courant*, "Shows the disheartening web of corruption that enmeshes New York, involving even the city courts." Even in far away England, the *Manchester Guardian* was quick to point out that, "The fate of Jack Diamond is without significance in itself, but the social attitude toward him is significant of much." In another edition it claimed that, "The American

Diamond being transferred from Polyclinic Hospital to Governor's Island. A. Ambulance; B. Police car; C. Heavily armed police.

crime wave was indicative of an international collapse of the west's social organization." Several other British papers suggested that America's crime wave was "due to the influx of south Europe's immigrants."

If Diamond's activities did anything, they focused the attention of the American people on the gangster problem. Almost every major magazine with a national circulation had something to say about him and gangsters in general. *Colliers* featured an article by New York City police inspector Arthur A. Carey on the murderous competition between gangsters. Even the usually bland *Ladies Home Journal* printed "Invisible Government," which told of the violence between gangsters, stating there were periods when between three and eight gangsters were killed in a week. In an editorial, in its July 19, 1930 issue, the *Saturday Evening Post* was particularly harsh on the police commenting that police everywhere had exhaustive information on crooks, that is revealed by the rapidity with which they round up the undesirables following an "outrageous affair." The editorial further stated that:

> The ability of the police thus to force large numbers of criminals from a city or to prevent their entering it is in itself evidence of expert knowledge of criminal haunts, habits, names. So the question becomes more pointed than ever. Why are decent people so at the mercy of a few criminals?

Discussion of gangster activity was not just limited to the popular magazines. The conservative and prestiguous *Nations Business* carried several pointed articles on the subject. One, entitled "Business Can Whip the Racketeer," discussed among other things the efforts of groups of businessmen to curb the racketeer in America, thus suggesting that American businessmen "interfere with the racketeers" who could eventually be put out of business.

5

The Big Cleanup

Harassed to the point of exhaustion, a pale, tired Legs Diamond retreated to Acra, away from the police, the newspapers, and his gangster foes. Gunmen, from the Higgins and Schultz gangs, were hunting him and the police in every big eastern city were waiting for the opportunity to pull him in for questioning.

His European trip was a failure and, consequently, his contacts in the narcotics trade evaporated. At the same time his bootleg empire was shrinking and needed reorganization. Above all, Legs needed money to restore himself and recoup his losses. To this end, he looked to the fight game, a popular attraction for gangsters of the period.

On several occasions in 1930 and 1931, Primo Carnera was a visitor to the Acra estate and Acra Manor House, a local hotel. Brought here in 1929 by Walter Friedman, a veteran fight promotor, Carnera was a sight to behold. He stood six feet six inches tall, weighed 270 pounds, wore a twenty-one inch collar, and size eighteen shoe. Bill Duffey and Owney Madden were quick to recognize his potential as a box office draw and became his American managers. Within nine months of his arrival here, the huge Italian went through twenty-four fixed fights earning himself a small fortune and national attention.

Kiki Roberts crying upon hearing of the shooting of Legs.

The exact role Diamond played in Carnera's fights is unknown, but it is believed that he invested a small fortune in some of the fixed fights. Diamond's interest in boxing certainly went beyond Carnera, for it is known that he had plans to purchase several acres of land in back of his Acra home for the purpose of training fighters. Although this never materialized, Diamond knew well or financially backed several up and coming young fighters who were guests at his Acra home on several occasions. The young middleweight Ruby Goldstein, also known as "the jewel of the ghetto," had lost only two of twenty-eight bouts and was a friend of Legs and a casual visitor to his home. He was once observed working out there and at times he would with his fiancee, Gussie Rosen, visit Catskill.

Diamond also made money from the slot machine racket, which he forced on unwilling proprietors of nightspots in Harlem and northern New Jersey. Abe Figura and Joseph Ham-

World Heavyweight Champion Primo Carnera in Washington, D.C., to discuss an immigration problem with Congressman R. A. Hartley on his right.

ley, two small-time hoodlums, ran the operation for him, fixing up the machines so that the house would get a 90–100 percentage instead of the customary 60–40 cut.

During the late summer of 1930, Hamley and Figura, backed by Diamond's gang, pulled several successful nightspots away from rival gangsters, one of whom was Waxey Gordon; this resulted in gang warfare in Hudson and Essex counties. By the end of October, however, both Figura and Hamley had been murdered and the slot machine operation went into decline.

The success of the local applejack industry was another enterprise that interested Jack. Local bootleggers were doing

Ruby Goldstein, leading middleweight contender.

a thriving business selling this brew that was actually a brandy distilled from cider. Diamond, however, was unable to learn the name of the biggest distributor in the area and called his gang together to prepare them for action. "This is a quarter of a million dollar a year business and we've got to get control of it," he demanded. "I don't care what it costs or how long it takes, but we have to find out who is pushing the stuff and knock them off." On April 18, 1931 he, Jimmy Dalton, Garry Saccio, and Kicki Roberts armed with assorted weapons including two sub-machine guns, halted a truckload of applejack in Jefferson Heights, just outside of Catskill. Inside was a very much frightened youth of seventeen named James Duncan and the driver Grover Parks, a small unassuming man with a slight build. Duncan was held at gunpoint, while Parks was taken to Diamond's home to be worked over. "I dunno nothin," screamed Parks. "Let me go, let me go." Parks, unfortunately, did not have the information that Diamond wanted and despite pleas of ignorance, was suspended from the limb of a tree in back of the garage, his legs bound by heavy rope. "You'll talk or we will beat you to a pulp," growled Dalton. Parks, his eyes wide open in a state of terror, again begged his captors to leave him go. But his cries were to no avail. The gang beat him about the face and applied lighted cigarettes to his bare feet. "Owee," "Owee," shouted Parks in screams that could be heard for a mile. Passing out for a few seconds, the gang left him to get some beer. Recovering quickly, he realized that his chance had come. He wriggled free from his bonds, running and crawling as fast as he could down the main road he managed to escape. Parks eventually ended up inside the Catskill Police station where he related his story to Chief George Klein and begged for a gun to protect himself. "Mr. Klein, you got to let me have one of those .38's or I'm a dead duck. That Diamond means business and if he catches me again he will blow my brains out without giving me a chance," cried the terrified truck driver. Klein calmed him and gave him a cup of tea, but the truckman was trembling so badly he could not hold it in his hands. "Don't worry Grover, you are going to get all the protection you need. I'll have the state cops in on the case by tomorrow."

126

Within hours of the reported kidnapping, warrants were issued for Diamond and the members of his gang. The details were carried by the wire services and the country had another major crime. The Greene County grand jury made quick work of the case and issued indictments against Saccio, Dalton, and Diamond, on a variety of charges from kidnapping to assault. Diamond though, was the only one willing to confront his accusers and he posted a whopping $25,000 bail, that was put up by the Grand Central Surety Company of New York City. The atmosphere in Catskill was electrifying with newsreel cameramen and newspapermen, from the big city papers,

New York State Attorney General John Bennett.

present everywhere. What would happen next? Would Diamond's gang get to Parks? Everyone asked questions.

Even bigger news was to be forthcoming. It was noted that aides of State Attorney General John Bennett were present in the courtroom on both occasions when Diamond was in court. Several newspapers carried reports that Governor Franklin D. Roosevelt was "watching with interest" the developments in Greene County. Weak, tense, scowling, Legs Diamond was obviously not bearing up well under the strain of events. "They'll never nail me," he boasted to Alice. "I've got friends in the right places and the money to control the politicians." Spending much of his time at the Aratoga Inn, just six miles from Acra, he waited for new developments. Owned by Jimmy Wynne, the Aratoga was a popular night spot that attracted visitors from all over the Hudson Valley and was a known meeting place for the notorious figures of the underworld. Typical of the roadhouses of the period, it was a huge two story wooden structure with a large bar and restaurant on the first floor. The eight bedrooms on the second floor were usually rented to transients or visiting gangsters. Large amounts of illicit whiskey and beer were kept on the premises and a still of considerable size was hidden in a shed in back of the Inn.

On Sunday evening April 27, 1931, Legs, Garry Saccio, Kiki Roberts, and several friends were drinking at the Aratoga's crowded bar, oblivious to the hired killers dressed in hunters' outfits who were sitting in a parked car just outside the front door. Legs, awaiting an important phone call from his attorney, paced the floor nervously. As he turned toward the front door to get some fresh air, the report of gunfire echoed everywhere. The loud bursts from automatic shotguns ripped into the building and the patrons ducked for cover. As the blasts tore through the enclosed porch door, one hit its mark. Jack "Legs" Diamond was shot down, for the fourth time.

The would-be killers sped away quickly, believing they had accomplished their mission. Inside of the Aratoga there was pandemonium. The bar was riddled with small pellets and broken glass, fallen plaster, and wooden fragments were everywhere. Most of the overhead lights were shot out and for a few seconds

128

Diamond being escorted down steps of Rensselaer County Courthouse by Sheriff Leland Grant, July 1931.

everyone was in darkness. Nine spent shotgun shells were found
outside the enclosed porch and a reporter, for the Albany
newspaper *Knickerbocker News*, later estimated that eighty-one
leaden pellets were fired at Diamond. The badly wounded
gangster was pulled to one side by Saccio. In all probability, he
was alive only because he was facing sideways in the dimly
lit doorway. Blood flowed from his chest as he writhed in
agony on the floor. Someone placed a bar towel over his
bleeding wound and loosened his shirt and belt. Within minutes
the Cairo town hearse appeared, for on occasions such as this,
it was also the town ambulance. Diamond was carefully placed

129

Diamond inside the Rensselaer County Courthouse.

in the rear on the hard floor and Saccio, with his big .45 caliber automatic stuck in his belt, slammed the door and shouted, "Let's go."

Rushed to the Albany Hospital at high speeds Diamond was put into the emergency room awaiting the arrival of Dr. Thomas M. Holmes, his personal physician, who was on the scene in a matter of minutes. The bleeding was halted but an infection set in and the gangster was reported sinking fast. Within two days a statement was issued that a pellet had broke Legs' left arm between the elbow and the wrist. Another pellet had glanced off a spinal vertebrae and splintered, with several of the splinters penetrating his lungs. One physician commented that Diamond had a tough constitution and a terrific will to survive. He was as tough as steel, for a little

Floor of the Aratoga Inn after the shooting of Diamond, April 1931.

fellow. For, in all his years in practicing medicine, he had never run into a patient who suffered such massive and continuous hemorrhaging in his chest cavity, yet was able to survive. Commenting further to reporters he said, "I had to tie off the vessels inside the lung which later collapsed, and then, as the wound started to heal, the lung was expanded by inserting into it a tube of air. The man is a medical wonder." For three days Diamond lingered on death's door. A three hour operation removed most of the pellets. One was left in the lung because of its location. Shortly thereafter, the infection and fever subsided and he was taken off the critical list, leaving the hospital after a four and a half week stay. Happy to be alive Legs said, "Well I made it again, nobody can kill Legs Diamond. I am going to settle a few scores just as soon as I get my strength back, you just wait and see."

The police hunt for the would be assassins bore little fruit. Captain William A. Jones, a nationally known ballistics expert who was brought into the investigation by the State Police, claimed that the shells found near the Aratoga Inn "bore similar spin imprints on the cap" as those found by state troopers in the barn in back of the Villa Pedro Inn. Catskill police, mean-

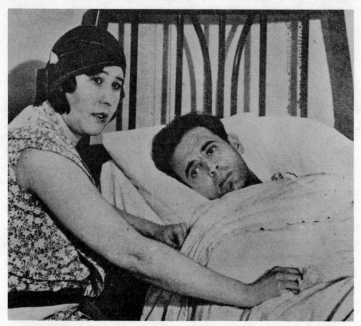

Alice visiting Legs in the Albany hospital, May 5, 1931. Note rosary beads over bed.

while, found a black Buick sedan on a town street that bore New York City license plates. Inside on the back seat, they found two shotguns and three revolvers, two of the three weapons that were used in the shooting. Those close to Diamond brought up the names of Spitz and Spitale, believing that there was a feud going on right within the gang.

The shooting and violence in the area prompted a number of

Catskill police chief George Klein examines bullet holes in Diamond's cap—a result of the Aratoga shooting.

Greene County citizens to ask for state help. Governor Franklin Roosevelt responded by ordering a cleanup of the Diamond gang and the investigation of illegal activity in the area. The Governor's intervention served as a warning to all gangsters in the state that criminal acts had got out of hand. "To Help Drive Band Out of Catskills and End Reign of Terror" read the front page of *The New York Times* and on the morning of April 27, 1931 dozens of residents of Catskill lined Main Street to cheer the arrival of the State Police. Eight black cruisers and some twenty heavily armed troopers sped through town to the county court house—ordered there to uphold the law and protect witnesses to be called in the Attorney General's investigation. Attorney General John J. Bennett began an immediate probe of Diamond's activities through a special trial term of the Supreme Court and the Grand Jury. At the same time, agents of the Prohibition Bureau set up their headquarters in the county and pleged to support Bennett. One federal agent enthusiastically told reporters that he was interested in bringing Diamond to trial on an old narcotics charge. He said very simply, "We are going to crush the gangsters in this area once and for all, no matter who gets hurt."

In an effort to determine who was working with Diamond, the bank accounts of one hundred county residents and officials were subpoenaed. On May 12, a federal grand jury indicted Diamond, Klein, Saccio, and Quattrochi on charges of conspiracy

Grover Parks points to the spot where Diamond and his gang kidnapped him.

and violation of the prohibition law. State troopers, in the meantime, raided the central beer and rum depot of Diamond's gang at the Aratoga and Villa Pedro Inns, seizing $5,000 worth of beer, wines, and champagne. James Wynne, proprietor of the former, and Thomas Carazzo, proprietor of the latter, were reported missing. Behind the Villa Pedro was a large barn that the state police believed may have been the site of the Western murder. The walls of the barn were riddled with machine gun bullets, possibly a backdrop for a target. State Police activity continued and roadblocks were set up in the area that netted several more bootleggers and small hauls of beer and whiskey. The feeling of uneasiness that prevailed was now replaced by one of calm. About two hundred Cairo citizens met in the local courthouse and adopted a resolution pledging their support to the police. Not since the War of 1812 had so many residents of the town joined together to meet an emergency. After an unusually noisy meeting they adopted a unique resolution:

> Whereas recent events, in the township of Cairo, have revealed conditions that the Cairo Chamber of Commerce and all good citizens deeply regret, not alone because of these events but from the knowledge that these conditions are not conducive to law and order and not to the opinions of the world at large; therefore be it resolved that the Cairo Chamber of Commerce puts itself on record as opposed to racketeering and bootlegging and calls upon its members and all good citizens of the township of Cairo to assist the Attorney General, of the state and other authorities, in apprehending all who are engaged in these unlawful pursuits, that the good name of the township be upheld.

The investigation was pressed, resulting in the opening of the safe deposit boxes of Diamond, his wife, and Diamond's aide Quattrochi. As the bits and pieces of information were gathered, it appeared that Diamond was much more prominent in crime than many believed. "Diamond gang link seen in eighteen counties," read a *New York Times* headline, while a one column write-up revealed that his activities were known in Canada. Phone numbers, scribbled on the walls of his home, and tales of big limousines coming and going from his estate, added to the story. By the end of May, 1931, it was known that he was

The Catskill Police Department, 1931. Left to right: John Fitz-simmons, James Fitzsimmons, Harry DuBois, George Klein, Donald Cairns, and John Healey.

part of a huge nationwide liquor combine. One newspaper reported that the state police and prohibition agents had under-taken the biggest drive in law enforcement history to clean up the stills and beer plants, claiming that "apparently the Governor's order to rip the Diamond gang out by the roots and destroy its chief source of revenue will do much toward making this politically dry district actually dry." The raids continued, with many illegal operations being uncovered in-cluding a $5,000 applejack still in Red Hook, in Dutchess County.

No one now doubted that Diamond's operations were big, but just how big wasn't yet known. Armed with information, from seized records, on May 1, 1931 prohibition agents swooped down on two large buildings at 35 Bruyn Avenue, in Kingston, and caught ten Kingston men busily making homemade brew. Close to 3,000 barrels of ale and some 41,000 bottles of the same liquid were confiscated; papers were found indicating that Diamond had a big interest in this operation. "It's a real big raid, with the seizure amounting to over $200,000, Legs Dia-mond really received a setback here," said one prohibition agent. The bottles of ale, labeled with the inscription "fancy imported ale," were ready to be shipped to the Albany-Troy area.

After questioning the suspects and inspecting the plant,

136

State Police roadblock on Route 9W near Catskill, New York, April 25, 1931.

the agents promised to continue their investigation as there was evidence of another illegal operation just as big, in the area, yet undiscovered. "We report all our findings to Maurice Campbell the Prohibition Administrator for the Metropolitan New York District. "These activities are too big and too well run to be left to local agents," claimed John Moore of the New York office. Unknown to area residents, three agents were assigned to Kingston to continue the investigation and put an end to Diamond's operations there. "The beer and ale have been coming out of that city by the truckloads for years, and hauled to the New York City and Albany areas," reported Moore. "But, where is its source?" His investigation eventually uncovered a large, flexible, two-and-a-half-inch rubber hose with brass connections that led into the Bruyn Avenue plant and

State Troopers and seized sedan loaded with bootleg beer, Catskill, New York, October 1930. Left to right: Sgt. Francis Hillfrank, Sgt. Howard Rice, and Sheriff Harold Every; the other two are unidentified.

138

went under the city's streets and sewer lines to the Barmann Brewery, about a half mile away, on Railroad Avenue. To avoid the suspicion of trucks coming and going, the operators at the Barmann Brewery had pumped the ale underground to the Bruyn Avenue buildings.

At 2:30 p.m., Saturday morning June 2, 1931, these three agents, concealed in the high grass near the Barmann Brewery, waited for the best opportunity to strike. Suddenly, a large truck left the yard and proceeded down Cedar Street when one agent jumped on the running board and ordered the driver to stop. The driver, it turned out, was John Sheehan, Legs Diamond's key man in Ulster County. Sheehan pulled his .38 caliber revolver, slowed his truck, and said, "If you don't jump off

Lt. Francis McGarvey of the State Police.

this truck, you're a dead man." The agent pulled his own gun and responded, "If you pull the trigger, you will shoot a federal officer. I order you to stop this truck and surrender." There was a few seconds of silence, with both men pointing their guns at each other. Then Sheehan stopped the truck and threw his weapon on the road. At the same time, the other two agents, armed with Thompson submachine guns, ran into the brewery yard and ordered the men there to raise their hands. Nine suspects were caught near seven large beer trucks in what was later termed to be "a million dollar seizure." As the men were being lined up a small bag of money, several pistols, and black jacks were uncovered. One agent, fearing gunplay, ran into the brewery office and phoned the Kingston Police asking them for as much help as they can give. Within minutes two patrol cars and four officers arrived, just as one of the suspects made a dash for freedom. A burst from the machine gun though, quickly changed his mind.

It was obvious to everyone that Moore's agents had shut down one of the biggest illicit brewery operations in the northeast, valued at well over a million dollars in beer, ale, and equipment. Seven trucks, with the lettering of non-existent firms

State Troopers from Sydney, New York barracks ready to do battle with the gangsters. Many of the Troopers in this photo were transferred to Greene County in April 1931.

on their sides and phony registrations, loaded with beer for the New York City markets were impounded immediately. The Barmann Brewery raid forced Diamond to make other contacts and start his operations all over again.

The Barmann Brewery, known for a long time by neighborhood residents to be involved in illicit operations, was also believed by several who frequented the plant to be the burial site for Supreme Court Judge Joseph Force Crater. The portly, middle-aged judge was wearing a dark, double-breasted suit and a panama hat when he took a cab in mid-town Manhattan

Grover Parks shows his son rope burn marks inflicted by Legs Diamond's gang.

August 6, 1930 and was never seen again. Crater's name had been linked to the dishonest activities of New York City Democratic chieftain Martin Healey, who extracted a payoff from Magistrate George F. Ewald for his position. He was, also, involved in several extramarital affairs and one young, wealthy woman was planning a $100,000 breach of promise suit against him just before he disappeared. Were Diamond's gunmen retained by someone to take the Judge for a one way ride? Did they bury the judge in the deep sub-cellar of the brewery? No one knows for sure what really happened, but his disappearance has become the mystery of the century, with several hundred thousand dollars being spent on the search for him.

The excitement over the brewery raids continued as more federal agents poured into Kingston. At the same time New York City Police Department detectives Frank Phillips, Neil Weinberg, and Chris Kelley registered at the Governor Clinton Hotel, awaiting the arrival of Jimmy Duffey and other members of Vannie Higgins' gang who were planning to shoot Diamond,

Barmann's Beer, from an early advertisement.

while he was visiting his associates in Kingston. The detectives hoped to catch the Higgins and Diamond gangs in one spot, before the shooting started. "It will be the biggest haul of gangsters in years, if we can pull it off," said Phillips who had worked closely with Johnny Broderick in battling the New York gangs. "We got a tip that Diamond will be here as soon as he can wriggle himself free from the custody of the state police." Sergeant James Simpson and four Kingston patrolmen were assigned to help the detectives and immediately searched the Orchard Hotel on Broadway, in the city, for any clues as to the whereabouts of the gangsters. The Orchard, known as a notorious hangout for bootleggers and the drivers of Barmann's beer trucks, was a place where tips on the trafficking in booze could easily be picked up.

As the weeks passed, the detectives and Kingston police decided that someone had tipped their hand. No gangsters showed up, but it was known that the gunmen of the Higgins, Diamond, and Coll gangs frequently passed through the city

Franklin D. Roosevelt, then governor of New York.

on their way to Greene County. Every law enforcement agency now seemed to cooperate in rounding up gangsters and their efforts appeared to bear fruit.

In the first week of May 1931, Paul Quattrochi, Diamond's top man in Greene County, was indicted for assault, for having pushed around a Catskill bootlegger named Joe Coglianese, and for shooting up his still. It was widely known at the time, that the tubercular Quattrochi, Jimmy Dalton, and several other strong arm men intimidated area citizens and innkeepers with machine guns and black jacks. It was also known that Quattrochi, Dalton, and Klein made many trips to Harry Western's Chateau, indicating that Ulster County was an important source for Diamond's beer. That, Western was deeply involved with Diamond no one doubted, for he had withdrawn $2,000, from his bank account, to pay Diamond just before he was killed. The Attorney-General's office verified, the well-known fact, that Diamond's mob had close ties with Capone's organization and other notorious gangs throughout the United States. Bennett claimed that Greene County was to become a nucleus for a gigantic organization, that Diamond hoped to spread in "a businesslike manner, across the state and perhaps, the nation. Indications pointed to his success."

Old Jimmy Wynne could remember well Capone's men coming into the Aratoga Inn to talk business with Legs. Capone and Diamond had much closer ties than anyone thought.

Salesman's card: Barmann Brewery.

GROSS REVENUE IN BEER
Full Barrel—31 Gallons

Size of glass in ozs.	Number of glasses	At 5¢	At 10¢
5	793	$39.65	$79.30
6	661	33.05	66.10
7	566	28.30	56.60
8	496	24.80	49.60
9	440	22.00	44.00
10	396	19.80	39.60
11	360	18.00	36.00
12	330	16.50	33.00
13	305	15.25	30.50
14	283	14.15	28.30
15	264	13.20	26.40
16	248	12.40	24.80
18	220	11.00	22.00
21	188	9.40	18.80
24	165	8.25	16.50

How To Figure Your Beer Profits

The above number of glasses can be tapped from a full size barrel of Beer containing according to the U. S. Internal Revenue Laws 31 gallons of 3968 ounces. Please note that although no allowance is made for the beer collar (or foam) the amount lost on the draw will about equal the amount saved in the foam or collar.

How to figure your beer profits, on back of salesman's card.

Phillip Thomas and a few others believed the Diamond-Capone relationship was built on narcotics. "Capone surely put up some of the money that Legs used in his 1930 drug-buying venture and probably bought some hijacked booze from him," said Thomas. "I can remember being in the kitchen one morning when he called Chicago to close a deal with Capone. Diamond mentioned several times that Capone was as big as they come and he was on his side."

Shortly after Attorney General Bennett's press conference, a daring attempt was made to break into the Albany hotel rooms occupied by Bennett and his staff, to remove papers taken from Diamond's safe deposit box. An unknown intruder spoiled his chances by stumbling over a chair and roused two residents of Brooklyn who were sleeping. In adjoining rooms were Assistant Attorney Generals J. T. Cahill and Henry Epstein. Also in the rooms were the Diamond papers that the investigators had

145

Unidentified little girl plays in front of the Barmann Brewery, Kingston, New York, just a few days after the big raid of June 2, 1931.

been studying throughout the evening. A mad chase followed that awoke the whole hotel. The intruder escaped and within minutes several state troopers arrived to guard the premises.

With a seeming determination to smash Diamond completely and totally, a long list of the gangster's lieutenants and associates was drawn up and handed to the grand jury. Among those subpoenaed was Marvin Parks, Diamond's pilot, who was really innocent of any wrong doing. He testified that apart from flying Alice, Diamond, and Paul Quattrochi to New York City, he knew nothing. He was followed by a half dozen proprietors of rooming houses, cashiers of two Greene County banks, and Thomas J. Carazzo, owner of the Villa Pedro. During the proceedings, word was received that the police had caught up with Garry Saccio, Diamond's muscular bodyguard. He was returned to Catskill and arraigned on a charge of extortion. Saccio, who had a record of eight arrests and three convictions, was known to be a terror with a machine gun.

"But, where is Kiki Roberts?" was the question on everyone's lips. For weeks, an intensive police search failed to turn her up and many believed she was dead. Then the news was flashed that she was involved in a holdup in a Middletown, Connecticut pharmacy. Three victims of the holdup identified her picture as that of a member of a band of three who took

The Barmann Brewery as it looked in 1964.

$127 at gunpoint. The only other important members of the gang who were not under indictment were Salvatore and Pete Spitale who lived near Acra, at the large summer hotel owned by their mother. Salvatore made many important decisions involving drugs, and with Irving Bitz, the New York City speakeasy operator, assumed a large role in Diamond's activities after Rothstein's death. Because they kept in the background, little incriminating evidence could be found on them and little was known about them.

On May 31, 1931, Legs Diamond was released from the hospital for the trip to the Greene County court house, in Catskill. He was escorted, by a dozen troopers to a waiting car which sped down Route 9-W with its siren wailing; along the way troopers, inside their patrol cars, kept watch for suspicious persons. In fact there was so much police activity that a visitor to the area might have believed President Herbert Hoover was coming to Catskill. Diamond's arrival was anxiously awaited by a large crowd in a carnival-like atmosphere that included newspaper reporters, newsreel cameramen, and dozens of armed sheriff's deputies and state troopers. To everyone's disappointment though, he was quickly rushed inside the court house by two burly state troopers, before photographers could get close enough to photograph him.

"They'll never get Legs," shouted a nine year old boy in front of a mob of state troopers, who were guarding the court

James Duncan (left) and Grover Parks (right) flank unidentified State Trooper, July 1931.

house. Housewives wanted a front row seat and crowded near the main door hoping, at least, to get the gangster's autograph. Heavily armed troopers patrolled everywhere, suspicious of everyone, taking no chances. Diamond's attorneys, though, sprang a surprise on everyone and after two changes in venue, got the whole show transferred to Troy, New York, in Rensselaer County. The legal manipulations and continued investigation into his activities had already prompted Governor Roosevelt to order an extraordinary term of the Supreme Court at Troy, to convene in mid-July.

Once again the preliminaries to the trial aroused great interest. This time, a star-spangled array of legal talent assembled to do battle in what was expected to be the biggest legal show in the history of the area. Diamond was defended by the brilliant Daniel H. Prior, a prominent criminal attorney and a former Albany city judge, and by Abbot H. Jones, a former Rensselaer County District Attorney. Saccio however, was not represented by Prior, which indicated that he and Diamond had

Grover Parks between two court-appointed bodyguards, July 1931.

had a falling out. The prosecution, which already included the State Attorney General and his staff, added Albany attorney Joseph Delaney and New York City lawyer Isaiah Leboever.

"We have to find a way to get to those jurors," Legs said to Kiki. "Either that or we got to silence Duncan and Parks, its got to be one way or the other." At the request of the Attorney General, extraordinary precautions were taken to protect Diamond, the attorneys, and the jury. Although Legs had four of his own bodyguards with him most of the time, Albany Chief of Police, David Smurl, took no chances and assigned six of his detectives to supplement the gangster's daily guard. Troy city police and Rensselaer County Sheriff's deputies were particularly alert for anyone who approached the courthouse without the proper authorization. Threats had been made to jurors and witnesses, and Harold Cluett, one juror, failed to report for duty, for which he was fined $25.

The fear that Diamond's associates might try to get to the jury or judge, was very real. Diamond's name was mentioned several times in the Judge Albert Vitale scandal, that occurred in January 1930. At that time Police Commissioner Grover Whalen had information that Diamond, Vitale, and the Sicilian gangster, Ciro Terranova conferred in a Harlem nightclub, while

Troopers Howard Rice (left) and Edward Updyke leaving Albany Hospital after serving a warrant for the arrest of Legs Diamond, April 1931.

Diamond was a fugitive from justice. Vitale, a judge in the magistrates court, was constantly under attack from reform groups and the press, for his friendliness to the underworld and the Rothstein organization, in particular. A later investigation by the Appellate Division, of the Supreme Court confirmed the suspicions of many. Vitale, accused of ignorance, incompetence, and of impairing public confidence in the criminal justice system was forced from the bench by court order.

The trial, itself, was surprisingly short with the state putting eleven witnesses on the stand, six of them identifying Diamond as being in or near the scene of the kidnapping of Parks. A trembling Grover Parks took the stand and repeated the story of the kidnapping, adding details of the beating and of his escape, saying that he saved himself from hanging, only, because he was able to grab the limb of a nearby tree. "My God," said Parks, looking directly at the jury, "you don't know these men. They are going to kill me. You have got to put them away." Mrs. Parks corroborated her husband's story and with a cracking voice, tears filling her face, told the jury that her husband came home with "a swollen face and bleeding hands." A vigorous, cross-examination, by Prior, failed to shake the two.

The defense was able to gather seven witnesses who claimed that Diamond was in the Hotel Kenmore, in Albany, at the time of the kidnapping, and despite attempts by Bennett, to undermine their testimony, they all stuck to their stories. Parks, in turn, was dubbed a liar, who had made up a fantastic story, so he might become "a hero and get his picture in the New York newspapers." The jury took four days to make up its mind and acquitted Diamond. A stunned Bennett stated, "I can't believe that justice has been bypassed. I just can't believe it." The editorialists claimed that, "It was a blow against law and order and an end to sanity in the legal system." The Attorney-General and his staff were determined to get Diamond and, to this end, they pushed for another trial on four indictments, arising from the same offense. But, by now, fear struck the upstate area and many respectable citizens lost their faith in the judicial process. Several Cairo residents, who saw Diamond in Cairo on the day of the crime, were threatened by

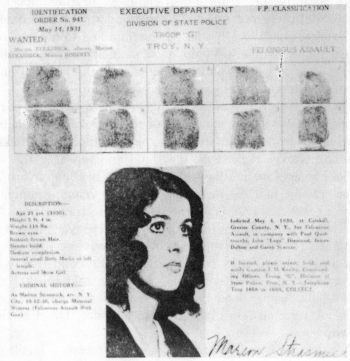

Kiki Roberts wanted poster.

machine gun toting gangsters to keep their mouths shut or get the worst. A few packed their belongings and fled the area. Even, in far away Philadelphia, the *Public Ledger* in an editorial claimed that, "Although Diamond was identified, by seven witnesses, as being at or near the scene of the crime, a not guilty verdict still resulted." Did Diamond's popularity have anything to do with this? The newspaper reported that there was no mistaking the sentiment about him. "He and his kind had become the favored symbols, of defiance, of an unpopular law. These same countrymen, who were the backbone of conservative law observance, cheered him and set him free. Obviously, the breakdown of the law includes more than the corrupt police and complacent judges."

Was Legs Diamond through? Was his organization disintegrating under pressure from federal and state authorities? Was his New York City contact still delivering the goods? Many believed that Diamond's good days were behind him, especially after, his New York City crony, Charles Entratta, was shot to death in his Brooklyn bottling plant by three gunmen. The photograph on page 162 shows Entratta lying dead on the floor of his office with a detective standing nearby. The picture being taken less than hour after the shooting. Entratta, alias Charlie Green, who was Diamond's partner in the Hotsy Totsy Club and in several other enterprises, appeared to be making a comeback in the world of crime. His main source of income was bootlegging, but he was known to have been involved in the kidnapping of several dishonest stock brokers who were later ransomed for big sums. He had a record of four arrests, at the time of the Hotsy Totsy Club incident, and his involvement in these slayings got him a twelve year sentence. But, he was later released in the summer of 1931, after serving only one year. Free again, Entratta, with Diamond's help, reorganized his Brooklyn and Manhattan operations, infringing on Dutch Schultz's territory. It was this move, more than anything else, that made him a marked man. Again, the police failed to turn up the killers. But their investigation did show that the gangster had a suite of rooms at the Hotel Ogden, in Manhattan, and was seen many times with a blond woman that fitted Kiki Roberts description.

Harry "Skunky" Klein between Troopers J. McNamee (left) and Dewey Lawrence, August 1930.

153

Harry "Skunky" Klein and Jimmy Dalton (without hat) being escorted down steps of New York City police station for trip to Kingston, New York, September 1930.

With most of Diamond's gang disposed of in one way or another, the residents of Greene County felt that they had seen the last of the gangsters. But the calm that had prevailed for a few months was rudely shattered. On the morning of July 19, 1931, two dozen state troopers led by Lieutenant Francis McGarvey and Sergeant J.W. Wheeler, six New York City Police Department detectives that included Frank Phillips and Johnny Broderick, and several area police chiefs and deputy sheriffs swooped down on George White's farm in Coxsackie, only a few miles from Diamond's estate. Trooper Harry Fritz, six feet two inches tall, strong and a dead shot, volunteered to

154

Left to right: Sheriff Clay Ferris, Trooper Harry Fritz, Louis Bifano (a member of Coll's gang) in handcuffs, Trooper Walt Wheeler, and Undersheriff Clarence Palmer. Greene County Jail, winter 1933.

approach the house first. Kicking the bolted door open, Fritz went straight for Arthur Palumbo who was about to take a shot at the trooper with his big forty-five caliber revolver. A quick flying tackle and a right uppercut to the jaw and Palumbo was through. The posse then poured through the main door and surprised eight men and six women, all members of Vincent "mad dog" Coll's gang. It was later learned that Coll had left the farmhouse just a few hours before the raid. As the troopers searched the premises they turned up a cache of weapons that Lieutenant McGarvey said was, "The biggest haul he had ever witnessed during his service with the state police." The weapons, in the photograph on page 158, were photographed with four of the raiding troopers just minutes after the raid. One trooper later commented that had the gang not been taken by surprise there would have been a big gun battle. "The Coll gang is one of the toughest gangs in the nation. They would sooner shoot first and ask questions later," he commented to the press. Proof of this came several hours after the raid, when state troopers broke into a garage in Cairo and found a bloodstained and partially dismantled Buick, which indicated that somebody had been taken for a ride.

The prisoners, including John DeRosa and Louis Bifano, notorious criminals with long records, were hauled off to the now crowded Greene County jail, where Garry Saccio and "Skunky" Klein were already guests. At the same time, word was received of new gang warfare in Manhattan between Diamond's associates and the competition. Among the first to be put on the spot was Brooklyn racketeer Myer Shapiro, a long time enemy of Diamond, whose younger brother Irving had been murdered a week earlier. The photograph of this funeral can be seen on page 157. The gunmen, who seriously wounded Shapiro, also shot it out with the police for twenty blocks before they escaped down a side street. Following this incident Tommy "the Harp" Sheridan, a long time friend of Diamond, was gunned down at 48th Street and First Avenue. Harp was known to have supplied Diamond with beer and was a frequent visitor to Acra and Haines Falls, where he was seen in the company of the most notorious New York underworld figures. Just before the shooting, Harp had been freed

Funeral of Irving Shapiro.

for lack of evidence after his arrest in connection with a $17,000 jewel robbery.

The presence of Coll and his gang in Greene County, indicated that there was an alliance brewing between the 23 year old gangster and Diamond. Both were implacable foes of Dutch Schultz and since February, Coll's gang had killed seven of Schultz's thugs; Coll lost his own brother in the warfare. The kill-crazed Irishman had also hijacked more than thirty of Schultz's beer trucks and this cut deeply into Schultz's profits. At the height of the trouble, famed columnist Walter Winchell reported that, "Machine guns and ammunition were flown in from Chicago to bolster Schultz's gang and the city could expect the worst."

Throughout the summer of 1931 the gang warfare intensified, until Coll accidentally shot a small child to death and wounded two other children in an attempt to kill a top Schultz aide. Eventually a New York County grand jury returned nine indictments against him. Seven of the indictments were for first degree murder and it appeared that the young Irishman was headed for the electric chair. His luck, however, was still with him and he retained the brilliant Samuel Liebowitz, the very same attorney who later represented the defendants in the Scottsboro case. After a hotly contested trial that received national publicity, he was freed and took up arms again against Dutch Schultz. The Schultz-Coll war finally ended in the spring of 1932, when Coll was caught in a Manhattan telephone booth and machine gunned to death. A short time later the remnants of his gang were collared in a state police raid at Averill Park, just outside Albany. Taken into custody after a brief gun battle were Coll's sister, her husband John Redden, William King, and another man and woman. All were known to have been involved, one way or another, with the killings of Dutch Schultz's gangsters and for the bombing of the Majestic Garage in the Bronx. Police speculated that they were in the area to contact the remnants of Diamond's gang, with the hope of forming a new alliance. Redden and King, already under indictment from the raid on the White farm in July, were granted $2,000 bail, despite their long records, and were released to await trial in Rensselaer County court.

State Troopers photographed with some of the weapons taken in the raid on White's farm, July 1931. Left to right: Eddie Updyke, Eddie Minehan, Harry Fritz, Howard Rice.

6

The Fifth and Final Time

"Gangster government is growing to such proportions that almost anything is possible . . . lawlessness has got to be broken up," said New York State's Commander of the American Legion. Echoing loud and clear, his words reflected the views of federal and state officials who went after Legs Diamond and his gang with a vengeance. By August of 1931, their persistent pressure brought results. Harry "Skunky" Klein, after spending a year in the Greene County jail, was taken to Clinton Prison to spend a five year prison term. Described on leaving his quarters as "a picture of misery" and "on the verge of collapse," he was approached by several reporters who asked, "What do you think of Legs now?" "Did you get a fair sentence?" Klein squinted, paused for a moment, straining at the two state troopers who were holding onto him and replied, "That no good son of a bitch double-crossed me. Look what he done to me. I'll get him, if it's the last thing I do." Paul Quattrochi was convicted of violating the federal prohibition law and for conspiracy, receiving a four year sentence and an eleven thousand dollar fine. In a prepared statement to the press, the tubercular gangster claimed that Diamond forced witnesses to testify against him, terming his trial a sellout. "That Diamond fixed everything up. I got blamed for things that I didn't even do.

I hope he gets his head blown off." Garry Saccio was next and he was given fifteen years at Clinton Prison, temporarily leaving Diamond without protection. At about the same time Arnold Green, an investigator for Daniel Prior, was arrested for trying to intimidate witnesses. J.D. Arglio, a close friend of Prior and a witness in Diamond's July trial, was arrested for giving false testimony. Flame-haired Kiki Roberts, sought in six states, finally surrendered to authorities on October 9. She was charged with aiding Diamond and his gang in torturing Grover Parks. A wanted poster of Kiki appears on page 152. Upon leaving the county courthouse the talkative, bubbling beauty said to one reporter, "Those goddamned, no good-for-nothings are always after Jack and me, but they'll never get anything to stick on us." Turning toward the big steel door of the court house, she adjusted her hat, pulled at her dress, and put her handkerchief to her eyes and cried.

In New York City, the federal government vigorously pursued the prosecution of Diamond and Quattrochi, for violating the federal prohibition law. During the five day trial, thirty-two witnesses were called by the 28 year old prosecutor, Arthur Schwartz, to prove that both defendants distributed intoxicating liquors and ran a 1,500 gallon alcohol still in Catskill. The amassed evidence showed that approximately fifty customers of Diamond, primarily local ginmills and inns, paid between $16.50 and $18.00 per half barrel of beer, the price in most cases being set by Diamond. One somewhat shaken innkeeper from Haines Falls said, "Diamond is the real big shot in distributing beer in upstate New York. Anyone that doesn't buy his beer or who crosses him gets taught a very nasty lesson. Just look at what happened to Western." The testimony of the innkeeper was noted carefully and deliberately by each juror who stared intently at Legs from time to time. One prohibition agent pointed out that carloads of Diamond's gangsters armed with all manner of weapons, especially machine guns and shotguns, were not an uncommon sight in Greene County.

Faced with such overwhelming testimony, the defense's case crumbled and the jury returned a verdict of guilty. Judge Frederick Hopkins levied a sentence of four years at the Atlanta Penitentiary and an $11,000 fine on Diamond. Paul Quattrochi received a two year sentence and a $5,000 fine. Diamond, poker faced throughout most of the trial, turned to Prior, "Dan, are you going to let these bums get away with this? What the hell went wrong, we have to get through to somebody, somehow." Prior, adjusting his tie and coughing nervously several times, arose and announced that he would appeal the verdict to the Circuit Court of Appeals and requested a low bail for his client. Diamond was released in $15,000 bail, which was part of a total bail of $57,000 in both federal and state courts.

At this time, the newspapers broke the story of a special session of the state legislature that amended the states' criminal code, as a result of the many legal proceedings against Diamond. Diamond had actually changed the legal process, a first for an American gangster. With so much alleged prejudice against the gangster in the upstate counties, Diamond's attorneys usually asked for a change of venue or an order staying the trial. Such requests were made to the Supreme Court, outside of the

Vincent "Mad Dog" Coll.

district where the case was being tried. The law was amended to require these requests to be made to the Supreme Court, at a special term within the district.

During the second week of December 1931, Diamond was again before the courts charged, according to Assistant Attorney-General Henry Epstein, with kidnapping James Duncan and assaulting Grover Parks. Prior's claim that Diamond's rights were violated because of double jeopardy were dispelled by Epstein, who stated, "There are two distinct persons upon whom these distinct crimes are alleged to have been committed."

The interest in the trial was without precedent and hundreds jammed into the halls outside the courtroom, waiting for the stirring melodrama to unfold before their eyes. The pretrial

Charles Entratta lies dead on the floor of his office. A detective stands nearby.

publicity was heavy, as the the state's newspapers gave coverage to every aspect of the proceedings. The selection of the jury carried a particular air of excitement, thirty-two prospective candidates filed into the courtroom and were examined but only three were selected. It took more sessions and the examination of forty-eight more candidates before the final jury was selected. Included among the nine jurors were a collar cutter, a station agent, a carpenter, a baker, a contractor, a railroad worker, and two farmers.

The trial began with Prior using every technique at his disposal to destroy the credibility of the state's witnesses. James Duncan, a short, slim youth of seventeen years, retold his story of the kidnapping pointing his finger at Legs. "That's the man, that's the man," he said in a quivering voice. "He ordered his thugs to stop our truck and then, they pulled us out on the road." Prior jumped up shouting, "Why you little liar. How dare you try to implicate my client in one of your farfetched schemes. You never saw this man before in your life and you know it." After twenty minutes of hard examination Duncan, now visibly shaken, stepped down. Albert Pierce, a former sheriff of Greene County, followed him on the stand as a rebuttal witness, testifying that he had observed Diamond in a Catskill speakeasy at one o'clock in the morning of April 16. Was Pierce's testimony bought? Many thought so including a close friend of Diamond who said, "Legs must have given him a bundle. He probably has the jury in his pocket also." Parks followed Pierce and supported Duncan's story to the word. Parks, a little man with a bulbous nose and narrow chin, stared at Prior who proceeded to tear right into him. Turning toward the jury he said, "you can't believe this man Parks,

> the man who tried to make a deliberate liar out of that dear old man Sheriff Every, the sweetest man that God ever put on this earth. Whom do you believe Sheriff Every or Parks? . . . Parks is a deliberate liar . . . I was prepared to show where Diamond was on this night . . . But I decided this morning and I convinced Diamond that the case presented by the people was so unworthy of belief that it wouldn't be necessary to call alibi witnesses.

How could two Greene County sheriffs give testimony supporting

163

the defense of Diamond? Faced with a possible ten to thirty year verdict, Diamond urged Prior to get to the jury and there is some evidence that one juror was bribed. Although they were sequestered, the jury was easy to approach during the trial and the juror in question was observed by a hired chauffeur, in the rear seat of a rented limousine discussing matters with Diamond and Prior. Statements such as this cannot be disregarded, as the not guilty verdict was against the weight of evidence. The jurors, primarily farmers and clerks just hanging on during the depression, could be influenced by a $5,000 bribe, more money than they saw in a lifetime.

After each day's developments, Diamond could be found in the evenings at the Kenmore Hotel's bar and famous rainbow room, Albany's most popular eating establishment. The one

Legs Diamond being escorted into the Greene County Courthouse, summer 1930.

hundred and forty foot long bar was a center of attraction in the downtown area, where burlesque palaces, vaudeville houses, and sleazy bars abounded. It was in the rainbow room that Legs relaxed with an entourage that included Kiki Roberts, several bodyguards, his current chauffeur, Daniel Prior, and Bob Murphy, the Kenmore's owner. Diamond's presence was usually the highlight of the evening for the pleasure seekers in the always packed hotel. Many just stared at him while a dozen or so lined up to get his autograph, on their menu. One woman from Hartford, Connecticut, who termed Diamond "my most lovable gangster," waited in line thirty minutes to get his autograph on an issue of the *Albany Evening News*. Diamond, of course, loved the attention and many times purchased drinks for admiring strangers. "I'm not worried about a thing." Legs said to Bob Murphy. "This is the last time Bennett will have a shot at me. I will come out of this mess smelling good. You just wait and see." Murphy, curious as to how Legs would get the verdict his way, asked the gangster, "How are you going to do it Legs?" Diamond turned toward him, grinned, and replied, "There are certain secrets every businessman has, I just can't tell you."

Tense, gulping water frequently, and nibbling at his finger nails, Legs Diamond awaited the verdict. He wore his lucky blue suit to the courtroom hoping this, his bribe, and his lawyer's efforts would pay dividends. Would the summation of Attorney General Bennett change matters? He had called attention to Prior's jocular attitude earlier, saying to the jurors,

> Gentlemen you can't laugh it off. The reputation of the county of Rensselaer is at stake. The intelligence of you twelve men is questioned by the one who says the law is funny.

The case went to the jury at 3:02 p.m., and eight ballots and three hours and twenty-three minutes later a not guilty verdict was returned. One newspaper reporter observed that Diamond was quite composed, as if he knew the outcome in advance. An outburst of applause came from the spectators in the court-room, while Alice ran to him and kissed him. At the same time more than a dozen reporters rushed to the phones, among them representatives of the United and Associated Presses, *The*

Vincent "Mad Dog" Coll and some of his gang in the hands of the New York City Police. Coll is at far right with mustache.

New York Evening Journal, The New York Daily News, and the local papers. *The New York World* was among the first to comment on both his acquittal and later murder saying that he was,

> Charged again and again with burglary, grand larceny, assault, kidnapping, and homicide. The sole legal penalty that hung over Jack "Legs" Diamond when lawlessness put an end to his lawlessness was a four year sentence and a fine for violation of the federal prohibition laws.

The *Literary Digest* summed up the feelings of most with their article entitled "Gang Law Beats State Law in the Diamond Case." As the reporters continued to grind out their stories Legs, Alice, Prior and his wife, Kiki, Micki Devine, a former professional baseball player, Dr. Thomas Holmes, and a number of others went to a popular speakeasy located at 515 Broadway, in Albany. They arrived there at 9:00 p.m. and began celebrating Diamond's victory.

As the evening wore on a new drama began to take place. Kiki Roberts was among the first to leave the party, returning to her apartment at about 11:00 p.m. Legs stayed until about 12:00 then got into a taxi, driven by John Storer, and was driven to Kiki's apartment at 21 Ten Broeck Street. He stayed there

The authorities look over weapons taken from Legs Diamond's gang. Left to right: John G. Cahill, Henry Epstein, Attorney-General John Bennett, and Lt. Francis McGarvey of the State Police.

for about three hours and was then driven to 67 Dove Street, where he had rented a large room and adjoining bath from Mrs. Laura Wood, with whom he was acquainted. At first Diamond had rented a Lancaster Street apartment, but had given it up at Kiki's insistence that it would not be safe. Legs left Kiki's apartment half drunk and was driven by Storer to his Dove Street rooms. Stumbling about and falling once, he finally got to the front door which Storer unlocked, putting the key in the gangster's pocket. Legs managed to climb up the stairs to his room, shed his clothes, and fall into a deep sleep.

Within minutes a huge black limousine that had been parked further down the street, in the shadows of some trees, pulled up in front of Mrs. Wood's home. Two men got out and went directly to the main door, where they inserted a key in the lock to gain entry inside. Going directly upstairs to Legs' room they then inserted another key in the lock of the bedroom door (or, as some believe, Jack could have left his key in the door), and pushing the door open, flashed their lights on a sleeping Jack, sprawled out in his underwear. Working quickly they grabbed him and fired three shots into his head. Both then bolted down the stairs but one, halfway toward the main door, wanted to return and fire a few more shots into Diamond, just to make sure. The other said, "Oh hell, that's enough, come on." Rushing down the steps they slammed the door behind them, jumped into a big limousine, and sped away into the night.

A few minutes passed and then Laura Woods phoned Alice Diamond, as she had been instructed to do in case of trouble. Alice, Storer, a Mr. Higgins, and Jack's eight year old nephew Eddie rushed to the Dove Street apartment. According to one reliable report, Alice rushed up the stairs and stood aghast when she saw the blood spattered body. "My God Jack, what have they done to you?" she screamed. "They killed my dear Jack, someone do something." Storer called for an ambulance as Alice wiped the blood from Jack's face, with a towel. Within minutes three police cars arrived, their sirens waking the entire neighborhood. The news spread quickly and the Albany newspapers put out special editions with the headline, "LEGS DIAMOND SLAIN." By nine o'clock, thousands of curious onlookers gathered near the Dove Street rooming house as state troopers and Albany police searched the area for clues.

The story of Diamond's trial and murder had attracted so much attention, that even the lordly *New York Times* carried the story of the killing on its front page. The *New York Sun* said, "His death was sudden but not a particularly shocking incident." In his hometown the *Philadelphia Inquirer* reported that, "Legs Diamond was Philadelphia's contribution to the New York City rackets, the local boy who made good in the big city." In a copyrighted wire story New York City Police Commissioner Edward P. Mulrooney said that, "He was not surprised by Legs' death, as he was no loss to the community, not to this community anyhow. I am not surprised. I expected to see him taken long before this . . . I expected he would be bumped off . . . and every time he came to the city I put a heavy guard out to watch him. That's the way with all of them."

Jack "Legs" Diamond had hundreds of enemies, each eager to kill him and this made the search for his murderers ever so complicated. In Catskill, New York he had made enemies by muscling in on the applejack trade. For a variety of reasons members of his own gang namely Salvatore Spitale and Paul Quattrochi, who was out on bail at the same time, almost certainly had placed him number one on their list. Irving Bitz and a host of speculators, who had loaned Jack thousands of dollars that he had never repaid, were known to be hunting him. In New York City, Vannie Higgins' gang had almost killed him once and was anxious to finish the job. "Get Legs Diamond," was the standing order given by Dutch Schultz, who was determined to have his revenge for the shooting of his close friend Joey Noe. And, of course, Alice Diamond must not be excluded from the list of suspects since her relationship with Jack was deteriorating and her jealousy over Kiki was known to everyone. Once she vowed to "kill that little bastard Kiki" in front of several of Diamond's associates, who believed that she really meant it.

The police investigation started immediately, amid wide public interest in the crime. It was believed, from the beginning, that hired professional killers were involved and they had stalked Legs for days. A police reconstruction of the incidents leading to the murder indicates that the two killers and an accomplice, who drove the getaway car, were waiting for Legs to return home from his celebrating. They knew exactly where Legs roomed and the exact room he slept in. John Storer, one of Diamond's chauffeurs during the week of the trial, first drove Diamond to Kiki Robert's apartment after he left the party. After a three hour wait, he drove Jack to the Dove Street apartment and returned to the Broadway speakeasy. When Alice received word of the shooting, Storer drove her to the Dove Street apartment and entered the death room with her.

Believing Kiki Roberts was the key to the shooting, Albany County, District Attorney John Delaney went to Boston to question the beauty in detail. Reportedly in seclusion with her

Dove Street house where Diamond was murdered, as it looks today.

mother, Mrs. Grace Strasmick, she always seemed to be available for the press. In one interview in which she sat on a couch with her shapely legs crossed one over the other, she smiled and joked with reporters, saying she was happy to be back with her mother and happy her mother had forgiven her:

I am sorry I didn't listen to her advice and because of this everything she said would happen has come true. I was stubborn and headstrong and I had to go out and learn for myself from actual experience. It was a pretty sad experience but I haven't lost my ambition and I have hopes of returning to the stage.

It was money and glamour, rather than wit and polish, that drew Kiki to Jack. The Follies showgirl from a poor home in Boston, had struck it rich, rich enough to leave Broadway and become a tag along with a big time gangster. "She's the sweetest kid in the world," said Diamond, who always professed his love for her and kept her nearby, right up to his death in December 1931. In an interview published in the *Boston American*, Kiki said, "Diamond was at her Ten Broeck apartment for only fifteen minutes." This was later refuted by taxi driver Storer, and under questioning by District Attorney Delaney she recanted, finally admitting that Legs spent several hours with her. When asked why she fled Albany, she replied that, "I knew they did not need me, as I could not throw any light on what had happened."

Kiki Roberts added very little to the investigation and the police looked to a multitude of other suspects, among them Salvatore Spitale and Irving Bitz. Neither was repaid the vast sum of money they had loaned Diamond in 1930 and were consequently bent on revenge. In November 1931, Spitale obtained a pistol permit because the feud between himself and Diamond had grown to serious proportions. Diamond, on the other hand, rarely carried a gun relying heavily on his bodyguards. In all probability the hired killers retained by Bitz and Spitale had been hunting Legs for two years and were the ones who shot him down at the Aratoga Inn in April 1930. State troopers who investigated that shooting, believed that the killers always had inside information on Legs' whereabouts and just cooled their heels until he put in an appearance. In an abandoned room at a farmhouse, across the road from the Aratoga Inn, they found the silhouette of a man painted on the wall that was obviously used as a practice target by the killers, while waiting to strike.

Further evidence of Bitz and Spitale playing the lead role in Diamond's murder came from information, in the hands of court officials, and statements by those who knew these criminals well. In March 1934, New York City Judge Joseph E. Corrigan, in sentencing Bitz to 27 months in Sing Sing for jumping bail, read to the accused gangster his probation report that included the following commentary: "It was generally understood Legs Diamond had been killed because he refused to return the $200,000 that Bitz and Spitale had given him to buy drugs in Germany." Five and a half years later, Irving Halpern, Chief

Dan Prior, Alice, and Legs just after jury's verdict.

Probation Officer for the Court of General Sessions said almost the same thing about Salvatore Spitale, who was sentenced to a term of five years in Sing Sing for grand larceny. District Attorney Thomas E. Dewey breathing a sigh of relief at the conviction said, "We can hope this sentence will bring to an end the long career of a notorious criminal, who has succeeded for twenty years in beating the law and has never before been convicted of a felony."

The hired killers of Bitz and Spitale always had inside information, from someone close to Legs. Everybody knew that whenever Legs was shot, Kiki or Alice were nearby or knew of the gangster's whereabouts. Kiki certainly would have sold Jack out, if the price was right and the dangers few. Alice, on the other hand, had loved Jack intensely and could not bear the breakup of her marriage over Kiki. The constant friction between Alice and Jack at the Acra home, and the increasingly lesser role Alice played in Jack's life added fuel to the fires of hate. Although she stuck by his side through many trials and arrests and was with him in his final hours, she knew the relationship had already ruptured.

The long romance between Jack and Kiki, and their closeness at the speakeasy celebration was too much for Alice, who believed that she had finally lost Jack. Crying to Storer, she wailed, "I can't take it any longer, I can't take it any longer, the both of them run off and I'm just left here, like I was some kind of a nothing." She rushed into the hall of the speakeasy and made a quick phone call to Spitale. The killers were then set loose again, just as they were before. With the information given by Alice, they knew the exact address of Jack's rooming house and the exact room he slept in. They were also aware that Jack did not have his bodyguard with him and that the landlord, Mrs. Laura Woods, would cause no trouble.

But, where was Sergeant Frederick N. Broderick of the Watervliet, New York Police Department, who was unavailable for bodyguard duties the final day of the trial although he had been Jack's constant companion for almost two weeks? He should have been with Jack, Kiki, and Storer in the cab and he should have been near Laura Wood's rooming house. Did Alice steer him away from his job, somehow causing him to stay at the

"Wotta ya mean acquitted?"

speakeasy that fateful evening? Diamond had first met Broderick, after an automobile accident in 1931 and offered the policeman a bodyguard job immediately. He was particularly important during the trial because, as a policeman, he could carry his weapons with him all the time and escape suspicion.

Weeks passed by and the leads developed into nothing. It was first believed that a motor vehicle inspector named Lyons and a cherubic priest, known as Father Carroll, may have been reporting Diamond's activities to the killers. Both were at the wild party, held at the Broadway speakeasy, and both seemed to have left at about the same time Diamond departed. A later police investigation actually showed the two to be legitimate citizens. Lyons was really Nelson Lyons of West Orange, New Jersey, a lightning rod salesman, and Father Carroll was actually

Door to Diamond's death room.

Father Norbett Carroll of St. Joseph Seminary, Calicoon, New York. Father Carroll had come to Albany with Lyons to confer with Daniel Prior about the projected purchase of some lightning rods for the seminary, but because of the trial could only confer with the lawyer at the party. One by one, the Albany police eliminated the suspects in the case but continued to press the investigation with vigor.

"Why don't you check out big mouth Hess, he could tell you a lot," said taxi driver Storer and the police did just that. Hess,

175

a prominent figure in Watervliet sporting circles and a brother of Eugene Hess, a clerk in Daniel Prior's office, cooperated but denied any knowledge of wrong doing. In an article carried by the *Times-Union,* Storer claimed that he and Hess went to Kiki's apartment to tell her that Diamond was acquitted, and on the way met the showgirl on a street corner. She already knew the good news and was preparing to leave Albany for Boston saying that, "She and Diamond were washed up since his wife was now back with him." Returning to the speakeasy, they went directly to Diamond and told him of Kiki's plans. "Keep that little bastard here, no matter what you do," Diamond roared, ordering Hess and Storer to her apartment. "Above all, keep her away from Alice, if you know what's good for you." A somewhat, shaken Hess and Storer, armed with a bottle of rye whiskey to bolster their courage, rushed back to Kiki's apartment. Hess remained with her, while Storer drove to 97 Dove Street where he had a couple of drinks with Laura Woods and her sister, Ethel Smith, then returning to the speakeasy. As the evening wore on Hess later went to the speakeasy and his part in the drama ended.

Some seven months after the shooting, the police received information that Edward "Fats" McCarthy was in the Albany area and he could provide a clue as to who killed Diamond. McCarthy was known to be a hired killer for the underworld and was easily available to Bitz and Spitale. For months, he was being sought for the killing of a New York City detective and for questioning in the murders of gangsters Vincent "mad dog" Coll and Vannie Higgins, and in the attempted murder of Dutch Schultz. On July 11, 1932 state troopers and New York City detectives located his hideout, on the Albany-Schenectady Road, and in a furious gun battle killed the gangster and wounded his wife and a fellow gang member. McCarthy's death ended any hope the police had of linking him to Diamond. His battered and bloodied wife, captured with him, was obviously uncooperative. "You no good swine, you will never get anything from me. Look what you did, you killed Fats," she screamed from the back of a police car. A check of the weapons taken in the raid proved of no value as clues.

The investigation dragged on into the summer and fall of

The room in which Diamond was murdered.

1932, but the Albany Police held little hope of a breakthrough in the case. One gun found near the scene of the murder was traced to a New York City man, who proved that it was stolen from him. Other guns, found several blocks away, also proved to be stolen, in fact, from an arms factory. At the time, it was pointed out that if a suspect gun was located, it would be difficult to link to the bullets removed from Diamond and the death room. The bullets had mushroomed so badly, that they could not be matched to the killer's gun. A New York City Police Department fingerprint expert could not find prints on the two guns, found near a flashlight, picked up near Laura Wood's home.

Just two and a half weeks after Diamond's death, Kiki Roberts opened up in a vaudeville act at the Academy of Music, in Manhattan. "See Kiki—the Gangster's Girl" read the posters and hundreds did just that, with the management predicting only success for their new found star. Alice, not to be outdone, hired a writer, retained an agent, and within five weeks of Jack's death she opened up at the Central Theatre, in the Bronx. Her brief skit was a short, meaningless attempt, to show that crime does not pay. At one point in the drama, she interrupted a mock holdup and faced the audience saying that, "The straight and narrow path is the only way in life."

177

With dreams of money and fame, Alice and Kiki took their acts on the road and in some cases, it was a rocky road. Unexpectedly, they met with opposition from the press, the clergy, and the actors who shared the program with them. In one instance the President of the Patterson, New Jersey, Minister's Association asked the police to prevent Alice's appearance, at a Patterson burlesque theatre, because she was "a woman whose only stage value is the fact that her husband was slain in a gang feud." In Trenton, a group of performers protested Alice's billing on the same night as respectable actors. "They can all go to hell," she screamed, in one of her hysterical moods, "they and that, that, low-down thing, Kiki." By late May, it appeared that Alice's road show was a failure. She returned with a heavy heart to Coney Island hoping to inject some vitality into her act by opening up in a ten cent side show that took the form of an interview with her, about her life with Legs. This, also proved to be a flop. Kiki, on the other hand, utilized her beauty and talent as an actress to put together a more exciting act. And she was still making appearances in the same town, where Alice had been, well into summer.

Beaten by the beautiful Kiki, again she was forced to consider new enterprises among which was a tearoom at Coney

Diamond's deathbed.

Grover Parks views Legs Diamond's body. To his left is Sgt. Hillfrank of the State Police.

Island. She also made plans to get a percentage from the sale of *Diamond's Widow's Racing Form*, which purported to have inside information on all the important races. Enthusiastic about these new projects, she moved into a small apartment, at 1641 Ocean Avenue, in Brooklyn. In the last week of June 1933, she was shot to death—a single thirty-eight caliber bullet entering her skull from the left side. She had been dead for almost three days when police broke into her apartment. Once again, clues were few. Her two pet pugs were alive but very hungry. A police search of the bedroom turned up a life insurance policy, an envelope containing a lock of Legs' hair, and a bank book that revealed Alice was depositing money at the rate of $2,500 a month in 1929.

"Alice Diamond Murdered in Cold Blood," blared the headlines and the tabloids had a field day, speculating that the gangster enemies of Diamond had finally settled an old score. The police, however, saw things differently. After a brief investigation, they arrested Edward Kenny, a former convict and "three-fingered" Florence Flynn, Alice's roommate at her Brooklyn apartment. Both were believed involved in the murders of Mrs. Flynn's husband, Lester who was slain in a Brooklyn restaurant on June 27, and James Dolan, "a friend and confidant of Mrs. Diamond" who was shot to death at a Brooklyn beer garden on July 30. Police believed that Kenny, who had the same last name as Alice but was not related to her, and Mrs. Flynn probably murdered Mrs. Flynn's husband in order to collect $5,000 insurance with double indemnity for accidental death. It was this murder they believed, that eventually led to Alice's death. Unfortunately though, for the police, not enough evidence could be found to pin it on the two and Brooklyn magistrate David Malpin released them on the motion of their attorney. The murder of Alice Diamond still remains unsolved. Though in death, she finally got to be with Legs without interference from Kiki, she was buried next to him in Mount Olivet Cemetery.

Epilogue

The semi-legendary figure of Jack "Legs" Diamond is complex and many sided, and one that changed throughout time. Those close to him saw a friend, a suave crook, a shrewd businessman, a wheeler-dealer, and a soft touch for a five spot. To the police he was a cunning murderer, a double-crossing thief, a bootlegger, and a dope peddler. He was other things, too, most of them mutually incongruous, a loyal companion to Eddie, a cuckold, a politician's friend, a gambler, and a sports enthusiast. He was a symbol of prohibition—a loquacious, egotistical gangster with a penchant for checkered caps, expensive blue suits, big limousines, and gorgeous showgirls.

Historically, Diamond marked the transition from the gangster of the streets and gas houses, who fought with iron pipes, steam kettles, and brass knuckles, to the white collar gangster, who turned crime into big business. His hand touched almost every aspect of criminal activity, including stickups, burglaries, kidnapping, smuggling illicit whiskey and beer, the protection racket, drug peddling, and murder.

He reflects what was then considered to be the American dream of easy money, fast and powerful cars, and an affluent life style, though he emerged as a persecuted victim of the police, in a battle to supply the public with booze. His exploits became legendary. His status and power grew to the point where he controlled breweries, speakeasies, nightclubs, up-and-coming fighters, and much of the narcotics and illicit whiskey industry in the northeast. He met with the lords of America's

Albany County District Attorney John T. Delaney questions Kiki Roberts. To his left is stenographer Frank Meyers.

underworld, including Al Capone, Vincent Coll, and Owney Madden, and with such European notables as Alfred Loewenstein.

To the public he was an invincible knight crusading against prohibition, and they followed his exploits with relish. The frequent shootings and accompanying trips to the hospital were always headlines in a city with circulation conscious dailies. In one issue of the *New York Daily News* his picture was plastered on both front and back pages, while the *New York Evening Journal,* not to be outdone, ran a pictorial display on him several times in one year. He was usually a prime suspect in many unsolved gang killings, and some twenty-four people were directly or indirectly killed by him, most of them in the most cold-blooded fashion. It was Diamond who emptied his gun at the Cassidy brothers and it was Diamond who arranged for the shooting of Joey Noe, as well as the thugs that tried to kill Eddie. Harry Western was shot from behind and his body still has not been found. Eugene Moran was shot several times in the back and his body was burned in the Newark City Dump. Within a few weeks of his death, his girlfriend was also found murdered. Walter Wolgast, the waiter who witnessed the

182

Sketch showing how Diamond was slain.

shootings at the Hotsy Totsy Club, was found in Bordentown, New Jersey, riddled with machine gun bullets.

Diamond was rarely successful in protecting himself and became a victim of gunmen five times. He was cocky, fatalistic, fearless, and undaunted as his foes filled him full of bullets. He was heard to say on occasion "they can't kill Legs Diamond," and probably believed this himself. He had a tenacious capacity for participating in violent acts himself and in the last five years of his life was involved in a whole series of adventures equal to any fiction hero. Some saw him as a product of his environment and his times, which forced him into crime, although he tried to gain respectability in a world that turned against him. A prominent labor official once commented, "Is it not a shame, that we find gangsters and racketeers entering the portal halls of our highest clubs and mingling with those in the highest strata of society?" Legs Diamond had the money, the thugs, the connections, and had even inherited Rothstein's empire, but still failed. Why? The answer lies in his psychopathic personality, which few understood in his day. Only in the past two decades has there been a serious attempt to identify and treat this type of disorder, which has been recognized for almost two hundred years. He clearly exhibited all the symptoms of the condition and was conspicuously different fom other criminals.

Like many gangsters of the period, Diamond died alone, leaving a wife, a girlfriend, and no friends. His funeral and burial in unconsecrated ground at Mount Olivet Cemetery in Maspeth, Queens, was attended by Alice, her sister and husband, three nieces, a cousin, and a dozen newspaper reporters. Several detectives from the New York City Police Department were also there, looking for suspicious characters—a fitting reminder that the gangster's dream was empty, futile, and lonely. Ironically, Dutch Schultz, who was shot in the bathroom of the Palace Chop House in Newark, was also alone when he died. And Vincent Coll was by himself, in a telephone booth, when he was machine gunned to death. Frankie Uale and Vannie Higgins were alone when they were murdered. One writer has appropriately said that, "in the deeper layers of our modern consciousness all means are unlawful, every attempt to succeed is

Bullets removed from Legs' body.

an act of aggression, leaving one alone, guilty, and defenseless among enemies; one is punished for success."

Apart from the numerous and greatly embellished newspaper write-ups, few knew the real Legs Diamond. Described as a menace to America and a ruthless, cunning murderer, he was still, nevertheless, a hero to America's youth. Wherever he went, young boys with sparkling eyes and outstretched hands sought him out. Many respectable and well-known citizens approached him in crowded places, to shake his hand or get his autograph. On one occasion, a group of Philadelphia's wealthy ladies organized a welcoming committee for him. By 1930 he was a celebrity, equal in stature to many national, political, and sports figures and could be placed on a list that included such notables as Will Rogers, Babe Ruth, Texas Guinan, and Calvin Coolidge.

Buick limousine believed to have been used by killers. Found in Summitville, New York, the night after Diamond was murdered.

Few dared to tell the truth about him while he was alive. Carolyn Rothstein in her book *Now I'll Tell* actually told very little about anything including Legs Diamond. Donald Henderson Clarke writing in his *In The Reign of Rothstein*, a biography of Arnold Rothstein published in 1929, did not mention Diamond's name on one of its 306 pages, for fear of reprisal. Though in his conclusion he accurately predicted that no one would go to the electric chair for Rothstein's death, which he believed was due to an accident. Some two years after Diamond's death Stanley Walker's *Nightclub Era* appeared, which discussed the Broadway racketeers and Manhattan's nightclub life during the prohibition period. In his chapter on Diamond entitled "Clay Pigeon of the Underworld," Legs is described as being a "frail, tubercular little rat, who was both cunning and cruel." Almost contemporary with Walker's book was Emmanual H. Lavine's *Gimme*, a rare little gem, which discusses the shooting at the Hotel Monticello. Not to be overlooked is Fred Pasley's *Muscling In*, which appeared in 1931. Pasley, who wrote the first biography of Al Capone, was primarily concerned about gangsters who muscled in on legitimate businesses, and the bootleggers who turned their operations into big business. Calling Diamond a "human sieve" he said, "Gangsters were shrewd businessmen, experienced in the peculiar Volstead processes. They went through bootleg war after bootleg war to bring order out of chaos into the hundred million dollar a year thirst industry, perfected their political tie-ups, and in 1931, were as solidly established in community life as a banker." Sam Curzon's *Legs Diamond* appeared in 1962 and was the first full-length, non-fiction work on the gangster. Inaccurate, it says little about the real Diamond or his associates. The reader will find such characters as Mary Bogen, who never existed, and events that never happened. Curzon picks Dutch Schultz as Diamond's killer, never mentioning Spitale or Bitz at all. He also relates the old tale that Legs was on Capone's wanted list for failing to repay Capone $55,000, which the Chicago gangster had loaned him to break the bank at Monte Carlo. Thirteen years later, journalist William Kennedy's *Legs* was published and favorably received.

Diamond being buried in Mount Olivet Cemetery.

Using the license of a novelist, Kennedy created fictitious characters and situations and sprinkled the book's 317 pages with almost every known obscenity. One Boston reviewer faulted Kennedy for not taking a definitive stand against gangsters. In response Kennedy said, "I'm not out to preach morality . . . gangsters are human beings and this was the scene usually left out of the movies."

The myth of Legs Diamond was finally extended to the movies in a 1960 Warner Brothers release, entitled *The Rise and Fall of Legs Diamond*, which starred Ray Danton, Karen Steele, and Elaine Stewart. Studio cards and billboards billed the gangster as "the hoodlum who rubbed out the ganglords of the 20's and built New York's most brutal vice empire." In big, bold letters in the center of one poster were the words, "The bullet hasn't been made that can kill me."

After more than forty years, Diamond's name still evokes thrills and excitement. He is the symbol of the bootlegger created by cheating citizens and crooked politicians. And he is truly representative of the wickedness of the prohibition era. His image shows no signs of languishing and his name is always a seller.

Appendix

Chapter 1

The Philadelphia newspapers, particularly the *Public Ledger,* the *Sunday Bulletin,* and the *Philadelphia Inquirer* are helpful for their descriptions of Philadelphia's districts and for obituaries on Diamond that disclose valuable information on the gangster's early years.

William Egle's *An Illustrated History of the Commonwealth of Pennsylvania* published in 1876 gives a contemporary account of the Irish problem in nineteenth century Pennsylvania. Dennis J. Clark's *The Irish in Philadelphia: Two Generations of Urban Experience,* published in 1973, is an excellent narrative of the attempt by the Irish to become assimilated in Philadelphia at the turn of the century and before. Some information on Legs Diamond and his father can be found in James Gospill's *Philadelphia City Directory* for the years 1898, 1899, and 1900.

The best source for crime in New York City in the latter part of the nineteenth century and the first two decades of the twentieth century is Herbert Asbury's *The Gangs of New York.* Other valuable sources are *The Police Gazette* and Edward Van Every's *Signs of New York as Exposed by the Police Gazette.* The night club era is best handled in Stanley Walker's *The Nightclub Era,* Craig Thompson's *Gang Rule in New York,* and in George Worthington's article in *Survey* for January 1929 entitled "The Night Clubs of New York." Charles G. Shaw's

Nightlife is also important for its descriptions of nighttime activity.

The most useful material on Arnold Rothstein can be found in Donald Clarke's *In the Reign of Rothstein* published in 1929, Carolyn Rothstein's *Now I'll Tell* published in 1934, and in Leo Katcher's *The Big Bankroll*, which is the most up to date biography on the criminal. *The New York Daily News* and the *New York Daily Mirror* gave excellent coverage to the Rothstein murder investigation.

Chapter 2

Andrew Sinclair's *Era of Excess* is probably the most authoritative work on prohibition ever published. Other important books on the period are Charles Merz's *The Dry Decade,* John Kobler's *Ardent Spirits*, Malcolm F. Willoughby's *Rum War at Sea,* and the 1930 United States government publication entitled *Statistics Concerning Intoxicating Liquors.*

There is abundant material on the gangsters in Paul Sann's *Kill the Dutchman,* George Wolf's and Joseph Dimona's *Frank Costello-Prime Minister of the Underworld, Bloodletters and Badmen,* and in Fred Pasley's *Muscling In.* Pasley's book can be singled out as an excellent commentary on racketeers and gangsters. Writing in 1931 Pasley sounded the warning that the gangster "will soon get such a hold on American institutions and politics, using corrupt police and politicians who already answer to his beck in the bootlegging field, that even the repeal of the Eighteenth Amendment will not seriously affect him."

Excellent accounts of gang warfare can be found in all the New York City dailies, particularly the *News,* the *Mirror,* the *Evening Journal,* and the *Graphic.* The *Graphic* featured write-ups on the New York gangsters. *The New York Evening Journal* assigned a full time reporter to cover Legs Diamond's activities in Greene County.

190

Several of Diamond's close associates are still alive and gave interviews that are especially important for the intimate details on the gangster's life. Phillip Thomas was Alice's part time chauffeur and bodyguard from 1929–1930 and knew Jack and Alice very well. Lyle Simpson worked for Diamond as a handyman and errand boy from 1927–1931 and remembered many details about Jack's daily life. Harry Morrison is a Cairo, New York paperhanger who spent much time inside Diamond's Acra home. Lloyd Tice played in a Dixieland band and recalled some of the popular attitudes toward Diamond. Police chief George Klein's interviews are important for the information on area police activities and the gangsters. Marvin Parks, Diamond's pilot, revealed yet another side of the gangster. Diamond's trips to many eastern cities establishes the fact that he was no small time crook.

State troopers Dewey Lawrence, Francis Hillfrank, and Howard Rice made valuable contributions on the role of the State Police in rounding up Diamond and his gang. Hillfrank and Lawrence were involved in surveilance and raiding parties. Both arrested Diamond at least once. Howard Rice was involved in the investigation of the shooting at the Aratoga Inn and raided several stills in the area.

Information on the narcotics situation in the early twentieth century can be found in David Musto's *The American Disease*, Leo Katcher's *The Big Bankroll*, and in Fred Pasley's *Muscling In*. Advertisements on narcotic base medicines can be seen in *Harper's Monthly Magazine* and in *Scribner's Magazine*.

Greene County residents and state troopers supplied much information on Salvatore Spitale. *The New York Daily News* and the *New York Daily Mirror* featured write-ups on Spitale and his partner Irving Bitz. The names of these two gangsters appear in several books on the Lindbergh kidnapping, especially Sidney Whipple's *The Lindbergh Crime*.

Lillian Cornelius and several other Catskill residents contributed information on Diamond's trips to Catskill, especially to the Catskill Theatre.

A discussion of the psychopathic personality can be found in Hervey M. Cleckley's *The Mask of Sanity*.

Chapter 4

Information on the Harry Western murder and subsequent search for his body can be found in the New York City, Albany, Kingston, and Catskill newspapers. Specific details on the case were given by Sgt. Dewey Lawrence, Sgt. Francis Hillfrank, and Police Chief George Klein.

Diamond's trip to Europe was a continuing subject of interest for the newspapers, especially the *New York Evening Journal*, the *New York Daily News*, and the *Philadelphia Public Ledger*.

The shooting of Diamond at the Hotel Monticello in New York City was again front page copy for the New York City newspapers and discussed in Emmanual Lavine's book *Gimme*, published in 1931. Lavine, a reporter for the *New York Daily Mirror*, was among the first to uncover information that linked the Vannie Higgins gang to Diamond. The reaction to the shooting can be seen in such newspapers as the *Hartford Courant* and the *Buffalo Express*. In England the *Manchester Guardian* commented on Diamond's activities and the crime situation in America.

Discussion of the gangster problem can be found in a number of popular magazines particularly *Colliers*, *The Ladies Home Journal*, *The Saturday Evening Post*, *Nation's Business*, and the *Literary Digest*.

Several newsreels of Diamond show him to be heavily guarded by police officers and always surrounded by photographers and reporters. One short newsreel, taken after he was escorted to the Philadelphia train station, shows Diamond with a pale, tired look; his left arm hung loosely at his side. In all cases, though, he is well dressed and talkative.

The New York Daily News followed his activities at the hospitals he was confined to after the Hotel Monticello shooting. A reporter was assigned to him full time and caught the conversation between Diamond and Cornelia Biddle.

Chapter 5

Gangster involvement with prizefighting was widely known at the time. Heretofore unknown information on Diamond's activities in the boxing world came from several items in the New York City newspapers and from interviews with Phillip Thomas and Lyle Simpson. A good picture of boxing during the twenties and thirties can be found in the *National Police Gazette* and in Nat Fleischer's *The Heavyweight Championship, An Informal History of Heavyweight Boxing from 1719 to the Present Day.*

The now defunct *Cairo Herald* was an important repository for news events during this period. It included some interesting write-ups on state police activity in Greene County and on Diamond's gang. The resolution adopted by the Cairo, New York townsmen condemning crime was published in *The New York Times* and the *Cairo Herald.*

The trial in the summer of 1931 was given good coverage by the *Catskill Daily Mail* and the Albany newspapers. The Philadelphia *Public Ledger* printed an editorial on the verdict.

State Trooper Harry Fritz was an important source of information on the roundup of the Coll gang. His heroic action in subduing members of the gang probably prevented a big gun battle. His recollections support other accounts that the members of this gang were ruthless killers and true enemies of law and order. State Trooper Howard Rice also participated in this raid and gave important information on the event. The New York City dailies, particularly the *Graphic* and the *Mirror,* featured articles on Diamond's activities in New Jersey. Gambling was permitted in many areas of Hudson County under an understanding between the authorities and the gamblers that the latter report any notorious criminals, especially holdup men and murderers, who came into the area.

Chapter 6

The Albany, Troy, and Catskill newspapers are important for the coverage of Diamond's December, 1931 trial. Frank Murphy, Diamond's part-time chauffeur, revealed in several interviews, many important details about the trial and the juror in Diamond's car.

Information on the shooting of Edward "Fats" McCarthy came from the *Albany Evening News* and from interviews with Sgt. Francis Hillfrank. The Albany *Times-Union* and *Catskill Daily Mail* gave continuous coverage to the investigation of the Diamond murder.

The *New York Daily News* and the *New York Evening Journal* are important sources of information in the murder of Alice Diamond.

Subject Index

Name Index

102, 103, 126, 135, 146, 166, 168,
169, 173, 177, 178, 180
Diamond Eddie, 17, 19, 21, 21–23, 29–
33, 38, 41, 48, 49, 51, 58, 61, 62, 65,
72, 73, 182
Diamond, Eddie, Jr., 168
Diamond, Jack ("Legs"), 17, 19, 21–
23, 29, 30, 33, 38–41, 44, 48, 49,
51, 56, 58, 61, 62, 64–69, 71–76,
79–84, 86, 91, 94–96, 100, 106–8,
110–13, 115–23, 125–32, 134–36,
138, 142–45, 147–53, 159–61, 163–
69, 171, 174, 177, 181, 184, 185,
187, 188
Diamond, John, T., 20
Diamond, Sara, 19, 22
Dillon, Frenchy, 55
Doyle, Eddie, 31
Duffey, Bill, 122
Duffey, Jimmy, 142
Duncan, James, 126, 149, 162, 163
Dwyer, Big Bill, 46, 48, 56

Einstein, Izzy, 46
Entratta, Charles, 51, 59, 60, 153
Epstein, Henry, 145, 162
Every, Harold, 76, 103, 163
Ewald, George, 142

Fay, Larry, 41
Fein, Benny, 48
Figura, Abe, 124, 125
Firpo, Luis, 33
Fleggenheimer, Arthur ("Dutch
Schultz"), 40, 45, 53, 55, 56, 68,
94, 96, 157, 158, 169, 184, 187
Flynn, Florence, 180
Friedman, Walter, 122
Fritz, Harry, 154

Ginsberg, Jacob, 118
Gruber, Al, 38
Guinan, Texas, 54, 72, 185
Guizak, Greasy Finger, 68

Halpern, Irving, 172
Hamley, Joseph, 124, 125
Harding, Warren, 29
Hart, Jimmy, 77
Healey, Martin, 142

Hess, Eugene, 175, 176
Higgins, Vannie, 94–96, 116, 143, 169,
176, 184
Hillfrank, Francis, 77
Hines, Jimmy, 51, 53
Hoff, Maxie, 68
Holmes, Thomas, 130, 166
Hoover, Herbert, 53
Hopkins, Frederick, 160
Hoy, Joseph, 105, 106

Jerome, Chauncey, 19
Jones, Abbott, 148
Jones, Floyd, 76
Jones, William, 122

Kaplan, Nathan ("Kid Dropper"), 23,
24, 40, 59
Kelley, Chris, 142
Kelley, Francis, 73
Kennedy, William, 187, 188
Kenny, Edward, 180
King, William, 158
Klein, George, 77, 106, 126
Klein, Harry ("Skunky"), 96, 102–4,
134, 144, 156, 159
Kushner, Louis, 25

Laimas, Abraham, 90, 91
Lansky, Meyer, 68
Lavine, Emmanuel, 116, 186
Lawrence, Dewey, 102
Leboever, Isiah, 149
Lebonatti, Roland, 114
Lievowitz, Samuel, 158
Lindgergh, Anne, 92
Lindbergh, Charles, 92
Loewenstein, Alfred, 87, 89, 182
Lombardo, Guy, 72
Lombroso, Cesare, 82
Lowman, Seymour, 53
Luciano, Charles ("Lucky"), 84
Lyman, William, 91
Lyons, Nelson, 174, 175

McCarty, Francis, 102, 103
McClaughlin, Eugene, (Red) 57
McDonald, Joe, 66
McGarvey, Francis, 154, 156
McKinley, William, 20